PATSY

The Roger Vaughan Library

COMING AGAIN
A novel, (2023) the sequel

COMING ABOUT
A novel, (2021)

LEARNING TO FLY
America's Cup XXXIII 2010 (2020)

DAVID
Ninety-Four and Counting - A Pudding full of Plums (2020)

ARTHUR CURTISS JAMES
Unsung Hero of the Gilded Age (2019)

THE MEDAL MAKER
Biography of Victor Kovalenko (2017)

CLOSING THE GAP
World Sailing's Emerging Nations Program

THE STRENUOUS LIFE OF HARRY ANDERSON (2013)

SAILING ON THE EDGE
(Contributor, 2013)

DROPPING THE GLOVES
Inside the Fiercely Competitive World of Professional Ice Hockey (2012)

GOLF: THE WOMAN'S GAME (2001)

MUSTIQUE II (2000)

LISTEN TO THE MUSIC (2000)
The Life of Hilary Koprowski

TONY GWYNN'S THE ART OF HITTING (1998)

NASCAR: THE INSIDE TRACK (1995)

MUSTIQUE (1994)

AMERICA'S CUP XXVII
The Official Record (1988)

HERBERT von KARAJAN (1986)

FASTNET: ONE MAN'S VOYAGE (1980)

TED TURNER: THE MAN BEHIND THE MOUTH (1978)

RHODE ISLAND: A SCENIC DISCOVERY (1976)

THE GRAND GESTURE (1975)

PATSY

By
Roger
Vaughan

Choptank Word Bank

Published by Choptank Word Bank
Easton, Maryland
www.choptankwordbank.com

ISBN: 9781733313582
Library of Congress Control Number: 2024925392

Cover and Interior Design: Joseph Daniel
www.storyartsmedia.com

Copy Editing: Elizabeth Cameron

PHOTOGRAPHS: Cover-Bim Newcombe, 6-Blue Passion Photo, 12-Murray Davis, 14-Peter Smyth, 22-Plymouth Herald, 64-Jacob Lofman, 115-Blue Passion Photo, 12–ROLEX Andrea Francolini, 121-Dan Nerney (2), 133-Murray Davis, 142-Graham Mansfield, 147-Dan Nerney, 204-Barbara Bradley, 238-Roger Vaughan, 265-Roger Vaughan, 293-Roger Vaughan, 294-Jim Kelsey, 297-Blue Passion Photo, 299-Olive Adshead, 302 to 303-Shane Couch, 304 to 307-Blue Passion Photo, 312 to 318-Will Broadhead, 321-Katharine Hauschka, 322-Kippy Requardt Uncredited photos are from the Patsy Bolling collection.

For Kippy

Table of Contents

PREFACE

Patsy Kenedy Bolling joins a list of rare, remarkable women who throughout history have succeeded at various dangerous and frontier-expanding enterprises, all usually consigned to the men's world.

Patsy Kenedy Bolling is a pioneer. She cut a wide swath through two predominantly men's sports in the 1960s and '70s: auto and ocean racing. She was accepted because of her skill, her talent, and her refusal to court favors. As one of her crew put it, "There was no feminine role-playing. She acted like one of the boys, and she was accepted. They saw how very competitive she could be—and how well she cleaned up."

At age eighty-one (in August 2024), Patsy continues to be driven by adventure thanks to her rigorously maintained fitness, her continued passion for and professorial approach to the sports she loves, and, some would add, a daily ration of rum. Her charm is innate. In one recent three-week period, she rode as navigator in a 1926 Bentley in the Flying Scotsman Rally in Scotland; crewed on a sixty-two-foot 1925 Alden schooner in the Antigua Classic Regatta; and survived a week-long celebration of her niece's wedding on Harbour Island, Bahamas.

The favored child of a roughshod Nova Scotian schoonerman who sailed freight to the Caribbean in the 1940s, Patsy's life is a compelling tale. It also provides a clear window into a rollicking era of auto and ocean racing the likes of which we'll never see again. She raced cars in Nassau in the 1960s, making lifelong friends of drivers like Sir Stirling Moss, Augie Pabst, and Dan Gurney. The list of boats she helped deliver or race reads like a who's who of legendary yachts. The wild parties she threw on Cabbage Beach on Nassau's Paradise Island will never be forgotten.

In the early 1970s, Patsy met her match—and her soulmate—in her audacious husband, Bill Bolling. Together they restored the 103-foot Alden schooner *Puritan*, among a dozen other noteworthy vessels. Fifty years later, after offering to share her knowledge of *Puritan* with the new owner and crew, she's become a regular on board, known as Aunt Patsy. *Puritan*'s owner was the driver of that 1926 Bentley.

I've known Patsy and followed her exploits since 1980. It's my pleasure to put it all together.

ReV

Patsy and Bill Bolling photographed in 2010.

I

PURITAN

Bill Bolling died in 2013.

Patsy Kenedy and Bill had been partners forty-three years by then, and it had been a chock-full, adventurous, often glorious, sometimes touch-and-go, mostly satisfying, always strenuous forty-three years. They were a combustible pair whose whimsical life together was about stretching the limits, with first one, then the other coming up with often outrageous notions the partner would rarely fail to support. Their relationship was pedal to the metal. Adventure-driven. Bill was known to yell across the water at some sailor whom he thought was being overly cautious: "Use it up, get more!"

Both of them were lifelong, blue-water sailors who knew how to restore, rebuild, and maintain boats (sail and power), as well as run them. Patsy had been crew on a 12-meter that had won the World Ocean Racing Championship (WORC). A fierce, talented competitor, she'd been

Patsy as crew on the 12-meter that won the WORC in 1972.

racing cars since she was sixteen, boats since she was five.

Bill was a renegade. After a few underwater missions for the CIA, a brief stint as a Pan Am steward, and a few years trying to work for his father's lucrative advertising business, Bill had become a Hollywood water-stunt man. His swimming ability had previously gotten him a scholarship at Northwestern.

Both of them had learned how to fly. They used their Cessna 185 floatplane like a car. Their homes were crowded with pets: cats, dogs, ferrets, rabbits, cockatoos, an ocelot, and, for several years, two Florida panthers that lasered the scary eyeball on visitors, and bit a few of them. Patsy enjoyed wrestling with those cats. Her forearms still bear the webs of healed scars.

When they came calling, they'd have a well-worn canvas bag containing their personal cups, a lime, and bottles of Brugal 88 rum for her—Luksusowa Vodka for him—not taking a chance the booze in their friend's cabinet might possibly be either of lesser quality, or in short supply. Having their own bottles meant they didn't have to hold back.

Over thirty years, Patsy and Bill had found eleven noteworthy yachts that had been left to decay, bought them for cheap, restored them hands-on with a working crew they actively led, and sold them for a profit. One of them, *Puritan*, a legendary 103-foot schooner designed in 1929 by John Alden, one of America's great naval architects, was unquestionably the queen of their fleet.

They had found the big schooner in complete disarray in 1972. It had taken them and a dozen workers six hectic months to revive it. They always presented the boats they restored by taking them cruising to upscale harbors, where potential buyers would be watching the docks. "Showing the flag," they called it. A remarkable beauty in her prime, *Puritan* redux turned heads.

The dream realized: Puritan *restored in 1973 with a bone in her teeth.* Opposite page: *Bill Bolling at* Puritan's *helm.*

Puritan had easily been the Bollings' toughest project. The job they did on *Puritan* was not worthy of a Lloyd's Register A1 rating. Lloyd's A1 is a coveted judgment made by the ultimate maritime classification organization. It's based on exacting detail of all aspects of a yacht, from design and construction to the condition of engine and rig to the perfection of gear and finish. But *Puritan*'s old glory was evident.

The planned sale of the vessel had been an enormous relief. Since then, *Puritan* has been beautifully maintained by a succession of several owners. "When we sold it," Patsy says, "we were so happy. We were out from under. It wasn't the money involved. Our co-owner was extremely generous with whatever we wanted to do. But we didn't think it was worth making her top-notch. No one knew it wasn't top-notch. Only we knew it. And the surveyors who found little details. But she was forty-five years old!"

Five years later Oskar Schmidt, the Austrian inventor who bought it, drove *Puritan* into the famous Camper & Nicholsons' boatyard in Southampton, England, and spent two million pounds on a complete refit—totally new deck, new masts, all new rigging. More than the boat was worth at the time. After that she was A1.

"It's true I had my doubts about the project," Patsy says, "but through the years I grew to have such fondness for *Puritan* because that project is probably what jelled Bill and me. And it fused the comradery of the gang that came along during those crazy *Puritan* months of hard work. They all kept in touch, and *Puritan* was surely the magnet." That was why when *Puritan* came up for sale again in 2014, Patsy's ears perked up.

Patsy was seventy years old when Bill died. Suddenly she had been cast adrift—not a very comfortable situation for anyone, but even more woeful for a woman with Patsy Bolling's energy, with her long history of completing with her partner what often looked like impossible projects. But keeping busy is Patsy's way. After selling the log house in New Smyrna Beach, Florida, where she and Bill had been living, she downsized.

Patsy, age 81, working to maintain upper body strength.

At eighty, she is a tough act to follow. On a typical day she's home from her five-mile bike ride by 8:30 a.m. She either rides around town or uses the bicycle she keeps at nearby New Smyrna Beach, which is broad and hard-packed like Daytona. She patronizes a gym where they have Concept2 rowing machines because she's worried about losing her upper-body strength. She'll often have lunch with a friend and play mah-jongg in the afternoon.

Never misses a cocktail hour. Rum, always rum. Frequent dinners with local pals or friends passing through are usually followed by shots of B&B where Patsy is living on the Intracoastal Waterway. One friend calls the busy place Patsy's Roadhouse. She tries to get to bed by midnight.

She has kept the "rum-offs" going, evenings when a male friend from auto-racing days shows up with several bottles of rum in hand, the object being to select the tastiest brand after careful and prolonged sampling and thoughtful consideration. Patsy more than holds her own when it comes to rum consumption. She claims she's never had a hangover. Since the rum-offs started in 2014, Patsy and her friend have passed judgment on more than 136 different bottles of rum *(see page 326)*. She has applied to the Guinness Book of Records to register this noteworthy accomplishment.

Patsy has also kept up with the yachting business. It is a lifelong habit. Her father, Louis Kenedy, was the last of the schoonermen who lugged cargo (lumber, coal, salt, Christmas trees, and plenty of rum) under sail between Nova Scotia and the Caribbean islands in the 1930s and '40s. Patsy wasn't quite born aboard ship, but close to it. And keeping up with waterfront scuttlebutt—"watching boats, knowing where they were and what was going on, what was for sale and how much," as she says—had been the foundation of the Bollings' restoration business for many years.

Seeing *Puritan* listed for sale in 2014 not only raised the hairs on Patsy's neck. It was unusual. The boat had never been publicly listed since they had bought it. Classic high-maintenance vessels like *Puritan* usually change hands quietly between friends and acquaintances.

She and Bill had the kind of stake in all their boats that comes with the commitment of hard labor: of fingers tender from sanding, of hair flecked with paint, of sore knees and too many cuts and bruises to count. All the boats they restored had pedigree. All of them had heart. All of them had deserved a second life, even a third. But *Puritan* was something else, a true thoroughbred, one of those unique yachting legends.

Puritan had been built in eight months in 1930 and 1931 by the Electric Boat Company in Groton, Connecticut. It was the only yacht Electric Boat ever built. EB had taken the job because with the stock-market crash, it had no work from the US Navy. *Puritan*'s butt-welded steel hull and riveted, lapped seams were a prototype for the submarines EB would become famous for.

It didn't take Patsy long to make a move. The day after she saw the listing, she cut her ride on the beach short. It was a gorgeous morning. The strollers and dog walkers were out. Dramatically backlit puffy clouds lolled in the Florida heavens. The view to the east from New Smyrna Beach is big-sky wide. Turn your back on the mainland and the flat beach stretches for a hundred straight-line miles to your left (north), and sixty more straight-line miles south to Cape Canaveral. Nothing but blue water lies between that beach and Lisbon, Portugal, four thousand miles a few degrees north of east. The vision inspires lofty thoughts.

When she got home Patsy wrote the letter she had been composing to the broker handling *Puritan*, a fellow named Mike Horsley. She didn't know him. "I wrote my name was Patsy Bolling, I lived in New Smyrna, and I used to own *Puritan*. I said, When you sell the boat I'd be happy to tell the new owner anything he needs to know. I have a model hanging on my wall, and some plans, and if they need to know the history I have a good sight on that. The broker wrote back saying, Wonderful, and I'll pass your name on. About six months later my phone rang. It was a UK number. I said, Okay, could be a friend, I'll answer it. A man introduced himself as Tomas de Vargas Machuca. He said he'd just bought *Puritan*, and the broker had given him my name. I said, Congratulations, I'm excited for you. He said, I'm excited to talk with you and I want to know everything. He kept saying he wanted to know everything. We went on for an hour. He said, Would you come sailing on her, and I said, Absolutely."

******

Nearly forty years earlier, in October 1972, waterfront gossip had it there was a big schooner lying up the Miami River unattended, in rough shape. Patsy found out the boat was for sale with an asking price of $120,000 ($650,000 in 2014 dollars). "It was *Puritan*!" Patsy says, with a shred of the old excitement seeping into her voice: "The old Alden schooner was on every boat nut's list of great, legendary yachts."

In 1970, Patsy was living aboard another Alden schooner, a seventy-two-footer by the name of *Ululu* that belonged to Bill Bolling. She'd encountered Bill at a few parties in Nassau in the mid-'60s when he was doing stunt work on the films *Thunderball* and *Flipper*. But she hadn't dated him, hadn't even been properly introduced. On Labor Day weekend 1970, she was supposed to be picking up her boyfriend, Mickey Spillane (no relation to the writer) and drive to Sturgeon Bay, Wisconsin, to join a race boat named *Yankee Girl* being completed at the Palmer Johnson yard. Spillane had just been named captain of the boat.

Patsy was one of very few women who had been doing a lot of ocean racing at the time on various competitive boats. For the few women who even attempted it, ocean racing in the 1960s and '70s meant being available to help with transportation, find accommodations, cook, sew sails, smooth out personal relationships, be an expert travel agent, and help solve a host of logistic problems in between races. But Patsy's car had broken down, and there were no parts available on a holiday weekend.

"Friends said they were sailing to Freeport, Bahamas for the weekend on this boat named *Ululu*, and I should come along," Patsy says. "They didn't say the boat belonged to Bill Bolling. They didn't say his wife and daughter were aboard. And it was a Friday. I never went to sea on a Friday. My father taught me that. It was his hard rule. If he had to start a trip on a Friday, he'd lie at anchor until midnight, then cast off. And I'd be the thirteenth person on *Ululu*. I knew it was trouble. But I went, and right away sparks started flying with Bill. It was a lovely weekend. Then I got the car fixed and drove to Mamaroneck, New York, where Mickey was. I told him he needed *Yankee Girl* more than he needed me."

She drove back to Fort Lauderdale and *Ululu*. Within a month, Patsy and Bill had become an item. Bill's marriage to Betty Miller, who had been Dan Rowan's sidekick on the TV show *Laugh-In*, had run the course a few years before. Betty had just been enjoying a proprietorial weekend afloat.

Penny Parrot remembers those days. One of maybe three female yacht brokers on the East Coast in the 1970s, Penny was living aboard her own boat, an Alden-designed, L. Francis Herreshoff–built (1936) seventy-two-footer named *Royono*, with her son, Jody, who was seven years old. The boat had been the flagship of the US Naval Academy, a favorite of President John F. Kennedy. *Royono* was docked across the waterway from *Ululu*, near Pier 66. "We

Above: *Penny Parrot steering* **Royono. Opposite page:** *In the 1970s, Penny and her good friend Patsy often raced their large yachts for fun off Ft. Lauderdale Beach with pickup crews.*

kept our eyes on each other," Penny says. "Just about every Sunday, Patsy, Bill, or I would see the other boat getting ready to go out, and we'd rush around pulling people off the dock to crew, and chase after them so we could race.

Sometimes Bill was away delivering boats. Then we were two women charging around in maxis. I can't remember how we made a course, or who won. We just sailed back and forth along the beach and had lots of fun. Afterward we'd have cocktails, and maybe a pizza."

"We ran *Ululu* aground one time," Patsy says with a laugh. "When Penny sailed past us we put up signal flags spelling 'fuck you.' She had to get the book out to read the message."

"Patsy is a very good sailor," Penny says today. "So was I. But I was a coward. She was so competitive. The one time I thought I could pass her, I chickened out. I was to windward, overtaking—two strikes against me. I knew she would have come up on me. I let her go."

When Bill wasn't delivering boats, he was buying, restoring, and selling them. Patsy jumped in. By October of 1970, the two of them had acquired a seventy-five-foot trawler-yacht that had been sunk. In three months the two of them had put it back together and sold it. Patsy's ability with all phases of the work, from sanding and varnishing to repairing engines, was impressive.

The summer of 1971 they helped Penny Parrot and her young son, Jody, deliver *Royono* to Maine. There was always fun involved on deliveries. Bill rigged a telephone he could make ring when Penny was asleep. A dedicated broker, she always startled awake to answer it. And there were other amusing moments, like when Bill was jibing the mainsail on a calm day by grabbing all the parts of the mainsheet and pulling in boom and sail. "Mom said don't lean on the lifelines," Jody Parrot recalls. Bill did. They broke, and over he went. A possible shark had been sighted a few minutes earlier, which gave Bill strong motivation to hold on to a small line hanging from the end of the boom. "He was literally running on the water," Jody says today. "Patsy was up at the mast, laughing her ass off." Bill had a rough ride, banging against the hull before Patsy could trim the mainsheet, bringing boom and Bolling inboard. The shark turned out to be a sunfish.

In the fall of 1971, Patsy and Bill had purchased a well-known race yacht, an Islander 55 named *Charisma*, from Jesse Phillips, a well-known racer who insisted on keeping the name for his new yacht being built at Palmer Johnson. They renamed it *Patrician*.

A less impatient, more conservative pair of sailors might have waited for warmer weather to bring the boat from way up the west side of Lake Michigan to Fort Lauderdale, a distance by water of more than two thousand miles. It was October. Snow had already fallen in Sturgeon Bay. During the day, temperatures might hit fifty degrees. At night they often dipped below freezing. "We shoveled snow out of the cockpit so our feet wouldn't get cold," Patsy recalls.

A slip at PJ's was expensive, but mainly they needed to get to work. They had a boat to restore and sell. The two of them cast off with *Patrician*'s seventy-foot mast lashed on deck, overhanging the boat by several feet at each end.

"It was one horrific trip," Patsy says. "It was cold. Snow and rain. The awfuls. Icicles were dripping off the gear. There was no electric working on the boat. We had one little oil heater we kept in the nav station. There were bunks on either side. If Bill and I were ever going to make it together, this trip was proof we could stand anything. It was a bonding of the relationship for sure."

The first night out they found a good anchorage. The next morning, the fun started. They had to jump the house bank of batteries to the engine batteries to get the engine started. Once underway, they couldn't make more than a couple knots of speed. The propeller had to be the culprit. In predawn gloom, with an air temperature in the low forties, Bill jumped overboard to check it. He had no tank, no wet suit. Just flippers and a mask. Making repeated dives holding his breath in the frigid water, he found the locking piece missing from the keyway that kept the prop from spinning on the shaft. Bill hammered a chunk of wood into the keyway. "That little piece of wood got us all the way to Florida," Patsy says.

The next night they anchored off Round Island, just south of Mackinac Island at the northern end of Lake Huron. What woke them was a wind shift that blew them too close to the beach. The boat, which drew only five feet, was dropping onto the bottom between waves, pounding. This time the engine wouldn't start. The mast was lashed into A-frames that were being lifted off the deck by the pounding. They had their hands full reinforcing the lashings. The Coast Guard responded to their distress call, and towed them off after insisting they leave their biggest anchor on the bottom. The Coast Guard towed them north to Saint Ignace, on the mainland, where they bought a battery they dedicated to starting the engine.

At Saint Ignace they heard stories about the 12-meter *Weatherly*, the America's Cup winner in 1962, sailing in the protective lee of oil tankers—tacking back and forth. The crew was unable to get the sails down because they were frozen in place.

Underway again, soot became a problem. "Soot was everywhere," Patsy says. "Everything you touched was sooty, it was a godawful mess." Bill ran the exhaust line and found a small hole in the pipe near the stern. "It wasn't so hot back there, so he chewed a wad of bubble gum, stuck it in the hole, and wrapped it. The wad of gum also got us to Florida."

In Port Huron, sixty miles north of Detroit at the south end of Lake Huron, they stopped to buy supplies, including long johns. One pair to share, because money was short. "We'd put aside eighteen hundred dollars for the trip, and it was disappearing fast," Patsy says. "With one pair of long johns you got to decide which was colder, your bottom or your boobs." They were also anxious about making the Erie Barge Canal at Tonawanda, on the east end of Lake Erie. The canal would take them to the Hudson River, into New York City, followed by a shot down the East Coast to Florida. The canal would close for the season in four days. *Patrician* was making five knots top speed with the wind behind her. And in November, the days were short—eight hours at most. "We had four days," Patsy says. "We figured we could make it in two and a half. We were so discouraged we went out and had a nice dinner."

Their timing was threatened by a foreign object that lodged itself in Patsy's good eye the next day. Her left eye has a birth defect. She had surgery as a child to make it appear normal, but from that eye she sees only out of the edges, not straight ahead. Now her good eye was too painful to open. "Bill said we had to stop in Cleveland. I said no. Every stop took us hours out of the way, and if we didn't make it to the canal on time we were really screwed. But he insisted."

In Cleveland the marinas were closed, but they ran into a guy who said he'd be delighted to take them to the hospital, where a small piece of rock was removed from Patsy's eye. She had to wear a patch for three days. There wasn't much she could do with it on.

They made it to the canal on time. As they approached the first major lock, they encountered an oil boom. A stranger rowing a dinghy helped them slip under it. Shortly thereafter they became part of a prolonged, heated discussion between Coast Guard officials and the lock keeper. An oil barge had sprung what was being called a slight leak. "A little oil goes a long way," Patsy says. "We'd been in a slick so thick it was damping down our bow wave and smoothing the prop bubbles in our wake. The hull was coated."

The lock keeper finally won, insisting that once in the system the boats had to keep moving. The barge was dispatched back to Buffalo, where it had come from, but not before the barge captain had given Patsy and Bill papers covering the cost of a complete hull cleaning, including a bottom job.

A few locks further on they came upon a dog swimming in front of them. In the lock! It was raining, very cold. The dog looked exhausted. Using the dreaded Jacob's ladder, a flimsy affair with wooden steps tied in to a rope, it was difficult to get the big dog aboard. They rigged a harness and used the main halyard winch to lift him. The dog was so shot he couldn't stand up. They bundled him up and fed him. The following day they stopped at a bulkhead near a bridge and found people who agreed to take the dog and find him a home.

They passed through Albany, got into the Hudson, and were in Jersey City, New Jersey, waiting for a break in the weather when *Weatherly* showed up under tow. "We had a good drunk-up with them," Patsy says. "Exchanged stories into the night. They had to boil water to free the jib hanks from the stays, and used a blow torch as well. They'd been through hell."

The plan was to stop at Atlantic City, then Cape May, go up Delaware Bay into the Chesapeake and Delaware Canal, then take the Intracoastal Waterway to Fort Lauderdale. It all proved uneventful except for Atlantic City. By the time they got close, it was getting dark. They were bucking into a southeasterly wind, and into a strong ebbing current from the marshy bays surrounding the city. Their speed over the ground had been reduced to less than two knots. Once again the mast became loose from the boat's constant plunging into waves.

"One of us steered while the other put new lines on the mast and used the winches to tighten them," Patsy recalls. "We'd get the stern set, and the front section would threaten to get loose. And of course it was raining, and very cold. It seemed we were making an inch at a time toward the harbor."

They finally got through the breakwater, and turned immediately left toward the marina. There's a very low bridge dead ahead if one doesn't turn left. They'd called ahead and been given a slip, but with the overhanging mast still on the shaky side, they tied up at the empty face dock instead of maneuvering into a slip.

"Very soon this very unpleasant man came down the dock shouting that we couldn't stay there," Patsy recalls. "Bill got his dander up and shouted back, saying we'd barely gotten in without losing the mast, and it would be dangerous to move. The guy said they'd assigned us a slip and we should go to it. Bill said he didn't give a shit, he was staying on the face. He was adamant. The guy threatened to call the Coast Guard to tow us out. They were shouting. It got heavy. Bill said this was a harbor refuge for us.

"I should have known from then on Bill was going to be trouble," Patsy says. But Bill was making his case. "He had the balls to write in my logbook," Patsy says today with a slight tremor in her voice. "In <u>my</u> logbook! He added to my entry about it being overcast but not too cold as if I were writing it: 'Just fixed my man a sensational breakfast.

Patsy with her 1955 Bently R, a gift from Bill after they sold Patrician *to Ted Kennedy. She sold the car for the initial down payment on* Puritan.

Afterward he told me how he had been reflecting on the relationships he'd had with women. Some he was compelled toward, like a moth to flame. Some he'd talked himself into, some which had very tenuous, unmemorable beginnings that ended the same way.' We had in fact been talking about those things. But that's him writing, not me.

"Then he started speaking for himself: 'But Patsy is so very different. There's the undeniable passion toward her, the electricity, the chemistry, but in addition it's the hour-by-hour joy, the fun of being with her that makes it all so lovely. To be continued.'

"Writing in my logbook, pretending to be me! Trouble. But kind of romantic."

Bill's entry in Patsy's log book.

Eight months after picking up *Patrician* in Wisconsin, they had put the boat in shape and sold her to Senator Ted Kennedy. He named the boat *Curragh*, and sailed it for fifteen years. And Patsy got a present. Every time they sold a boat she would get a gift from Bill. For *Patrician*, it was a 1955 Bentley R. "I wouldn't have it for long," she says.

******

The very day Patsy and Bill heard the rumor about a big schooner left to decay up the Miami River, they went to see it. What greeted them was ugly. "It was bittersweet," Patsy says. "Sweet because no amount of age or mistreatment could hide those lovely lines, the thoroughbred pedigree, the instant sense that this creation was a near-perfect specimen of a yacht capable of handling whatever the oceans of the world could throw at her. Bitter because the mistreatment had been extreme, abusive. It made the bile of anger rise up in the throat that such a thing of beauty could have been so trashed, so neglected. Rust was everywhere. The decks were warped and sprung. Brightwork was a memory. Hatches were stuck open, the wheel was broken, halyard ends were frayed, rigging was twisted and coming apart. The only sail bent on was the forestaysail, and it was rotten. Grass and small trees were growing in the scuppers and waterways. We were stunned. It was a lot to take in. We were rooted in place, staring. Bill and I must have let our eyes wander over the wreckage for more than a minute, saying nothing. Then we looked at one another, our eyes still smarting, and an odd thing happened: we laughed, but for different reasons. Bill had seen the sweet. Bill said we could do this. I wasn't so sure."

Below deck was more of the same. The carpets were squishy with water. Doors and cabinets were soaked and swollen shut. The engine room was trashed beyond belief with rust and corrosion. Nothing worked. The galley was a dark, dirty hole. It was so depressing. There was no electric aboard; not even shore power worked. The smell of decay was powerful.

While Bill was immediately intrigued by the boat, Patsy says she was groaning at the very thought of taking on *Puritan*. A restoration looked totally daunting, impossible. "I have to admit the more I thought about it, the more I couldn't believe Bill would even think of doing it. I couldn't see his vision at all." Previous vessels they'd restored were smaller, more modern. Here was a classic yacht that would need parts difficult to find, a forty-year-old yacht that would require a lot of traditional treatment. And the finances were way out of their league. But Bill was starry-eyed.

Patsy told her friend Penny what they were contemplating, and asked her to broker the deal. "Patsy came to me," Penny says, "told me they wanted to buy this boat. I went to have a look and saw this rusty old hulk sitting in the mud. I told Patsy, This thing is a piece of shit, are you crazy? They persisted. I went to see it again. I knew Patsy was a hell of a sailor with a great eye. Maybe I was being too hasty. But no, it was beyond belief. So full of rust on deck and below. I would have scuttled her. I said, You guys are crazy. I can't do it. They went to another broker."

Their offer of $75,000 was accepted. The only problem was where they would find the money. They made a small dent by selling Patsy's Bentley R for $7,500. Then they put word out on the waterfront telegraph that a financial partner was needed. They were just as accomplished at that end of the business as they were at the restoration. Bill could have sold ice to Inuits. And Patsy seems to have been born charming, a virtue polished from the time she was a cute blonde five-year-old girl accompanying her doting, two-fisted father to seamen's bars in Nova Scotia, where she was raised. Together, Patsy and Bill were a tough act to ignore—so Chicagoan Gerald Gidwitz found out when he had the temerity to respond about the partnership being offered.

Gidwitz was no slouch himself when it came to smoke and mirrors. He and a friend had founded Helene Curtis cosmetics with clay dug out of the Arkansas River bank and attractively packaged as Peach Bloom Facial Mask. Gidwitz was regarded more as an entrepreneur focused on acquisitions and side businesses than as a master of cosmetics. He was sixty-three years old when he first came to visit the schooner. To be fair, he knew nothing of boats and the water. He was just a very wealthy man looking for adventure.

Raynell Courten (now Raynell Smith), a former high school teacher who was one of the early hires for the *Puritan* restoration crew, remembers the day when Gidwitz came to visit: "Bill was walking him up and down the deck. Mr. Gidwitz was wearing his white athletic socks, which was a riot because it was quite slippery. Bill was sweet-talking him, telling him stories, and making sure he had the best possible time. Bill had that ability."

Gidwitz turned out to be a partner from heaven. He not only put up most of the money to buy the boat but insisted Patsy and Bill be treated as fifty-fifty partners. He provided a salary during the restoration and, when they began sailing, a better salary as captain and mate. Every time he was on board, he paid a charter fee, plus providing food, fuel, and dockage.

"He was the original medicine man," Patsy says, "a snake-oil salesman. He and Bill got along famously. There were never any questions. It was a little rough in the beginning because Gidwitz's lawyers were taking good care of him. We said, Oh my God, can we do all this stuff? Gidwitz said, Hell, just sign the bloody papers and get on with it. We were skeptical at first. We didn't know the guy. There were a lot of faith and handshakes involved. But it was all good. He stuck to us like shit to a blanket."

In December, just two months after they'd first laid eyes on the boat, *Puritan* was hauled out at Merrill-Stevens shipyard in Miami for a survey, and to have a ton of mud and marine growth scraped off her steel hull. With the boat back in the water, a mechanic spent days reviving the yacht's GM 8v71 diesel engine, while Bill and others filtered fuel and assisted. On deck, Patsy, Penny Parrot, and other friends cleared the waterways, swept the deck, organized the rigging, and glued the wheel back together. Down below, they managed to get one head working. Using shore power, they cleaned and charged *Puritan*'s batteries. Yes, Penny helped. She'd refused to facilitate a sale she hadn't believed in, but once the boat had been sold, friendship prevailed.

Patsy and Bill had that kind of magnetism. With them leading the pack, there was fun to be had, rum to be drunk, adventures lying ahead.

The object was to move *Puritan* forty miles north to River Bend Marina, a small yard up the New River in Fort Lauderdale. The owner had welcomed the refit of the big schooner as an attraction, and had offered Patsy and Bill a handsome deal. There was just one sticky problem. In the two years since *Puritan* had been left at Merrill-Stevens, I-95 had been built over the Miami River. The bridge clearance at mean low water was listed at seventy-five feet, the exact height of *Puritan*'s mainmast off the water. If that seems short for a 103-foot yacht, remember the yacht is gaff rigged, a configuration adding significantly to the height—and size—of the mainsail. And the topmast was housed (not in place).

On a Sunday, with fair weather and a moderate breeze, with crew, family, and friends numbering ten, the foresail was bent on and *Puritan* got underway. It was dead low tide. A man went aloft as they approached the I-95 bridge, and all eyes turned skyward. "It's close!" the mast man shouted as *Puritan* inched toward the bridge. "Not gonna make it, wait, maybe, a little more left, oh man, reverse!—no, go ahead . . ." He ducked his head as the cap of the mainmast cleared by inches.

"We set what sail we had," Patsy recalls, "the fore and forestays'l. Both were tattered and torn, but they held in the light breeze. We eased along with the engine barely turning over. *Puritan* came alive for the first time in years as we headed for Fort Lauderdale." But she sailed poorly because the centerboard was stuck in the up position. A small tug helped them negotiate the channel up to River Bend. Six feet from the undersized dock the vessel ran aground, just close enough for a gangplank to bridge the gap. *Puritan* settled into a hole of her own making. The work would begin the next day.

Lou Kenedy and daughter Patsy with a model of **Wawaloam,** *Lou's schooner that was sunk by a German U-boat.*

II

LOU

Patsy Kenedy was born in 1943 in Conquerall Bank, Nova Scotia, a crossroads seventy miles west of Halifax on the LaHave River. Population of Conquerall Bank was around three hundred at the time. She was Louis and Patricia Kenedy's second child. Brian was her older brother. Sisters Gabrielle (Gay) and Rosemary (Rosie) would follow. "After Daddy got home from being torpedoed," Patsy says with a chuckle, "there was lots of fucking going on."

Lou Kenedy was the dominant figure in Patsy's childhood, in her life. He was already something of a legend by the time she was born. "Patsy, Gabrielle, and I lived through the stories, and they never got old," her sister Rosie says today. "Some of the tales were so tall you'd

Patsy, at twenty-three, helping her father stock essential items for a charter cruise. She began crewing on his various boats at age eleven.

think they had to be made up. But later on in life you hear little bits and you realize they weren't exaggerated. Nothing was made up.

"One time I was pulling into an FBO in Eleuthera and the man said, You Lou Kenedy's daughter? I said yes, and he said, When I was a little boy I was on his boat in Spanish Wells and I saw him eat a can of dog food. He did it for customs. He had a whole bunch of Alpo he was smuggling in for people—and the customs guy said, What's all this dog food, what are you taking all this for? And Lou said, Dog food? This is horse meat! Good horse meat. And he opened a can and started eating it. When I first heard that story I thought it was a bunch of bull. Thirty years later I run into a guy who was practically traumatized by seeing my father do it."

FBO is short for fixed-base operator, a group authorized to sell fuel and provide other services at airports. Rosie had been a frequent visitor to FBOs when she was living on Sampson Cay, a thirty-acre island sixty-five miles southeast of Nassau that she and her husband had leased from the government. They were in the marine-salvage business. Rosie's husband, Marcus Mitchell, was away a lot on business. Building a school for her four kids, tending bar, unloading fuel, and keeping the books kept her busy at home. She and Marcus each had a floatplane.

"I was insecure about transportation when Marcus was away," Rosie says. "But people who learn to walk on a boat don't necessarily like airplanes. I had to face my fear. I went away for two months when Marcus was home, without his blessing, and learned to fly a plane. Got a license. Got my seaplane rating. Went back. Marcus bought a new plane, I got to use the old one. I realized I just got a license to go out and kill myself unless I practiced. I practiced. I used to promise God I'd be a nun every time I got in the plane if I survived, but he rejected me. He didn't want me. I was too used up. Little by little I started to fall in love with it."

As kids, Patsy and Rosie were capable tomboys ready to tackle whatever came along. "Barefoot, bushy-tailed, and no bra," Patsy says. "I didn't wear a bra until I was seventy." Gabrielle, the middle sister, was more into fashion than sports. "Gay was the girly girl among us," Rosie says. "Attractive, warm, always dressed to the nines. She did a lot of modeling in Nassau." Gabrielle currently lives in Nassau with her youngest daughter, Sabrina, under memory care.

******

Lou's family was wealthy. They owned P. J. Kenedy & Sons, one of the largest publishers of Catholic books and directories in the country in the 1930s. P. J. Kenedy was associated with the Holy See in Rome. The family lived in New Rochelle and Pelham, New York. They had a cottage on fashionable Schroon Lake in the Adirondacks. Lou's father was a flag officer of the Huguenot Yacht Club in New Rochelle. Lou's early years were typical for a boy born into his situation. He had an early attraction to boats. He raced in the competitive Star and 6-meter classes with top skippers like Briggs Cunningham and Olin Stephens. When he was just fourteen he bought a twenty-five-foot Friendship sloop in need of work, played hooky to fix it up, and cruised long distances with his pals, bumming lobsters from fishing boats and stealing corn from fields. He spent one year at Georgetown University before he decided college, and a career in Catholic publishing, was not for him.

"His old man was strict, very stern," Patsy says. "He didn't like Lou leaving, but Lou was eighteen, and he inherited a bundle of his great-grandfather's adventure-bound, controlling genes. Lou challenged his father's wishes. When he'd come home weekends, his mother or grandmom would slip him money. Then he just went to sea."

The late Joe Russell's engaging book *The Last Schoonerman: The Remarkable Life of Captain Lou Kenedy* reads like a maritime tale of misadventures, mistakes, bad luck, frugality in the extreme, overreactions, and, at times, plain bullheadedness mixed with a stout heart, an immense dose of courage, and a determined way of surviving. Somehow, it has a happy ending. It begins in 1928 with Lou, a tall, robust kid of eighteen offering himself as crew to the roughneck skipper of a Chesapeake bugeye. When told to cook beans for the crew, Lou put too many in the pot and had to sneak the lot overboard.

By the age of twenty-one, Lou had earned his master's license and was off (in his Stutz Bearcat) to buy his first old schooner, a 138-footer named *Abundance* requiring one hundred strokes several times a day on the bilge pump. He was in such a rush to see the boat that he refused to stop for his traveling companion to pee, or to eat. He had a short temper. When one of the *Abundance*'s crew challenged Lou, saying he wouldn't work until he got a raise, Lou pulled a pistol on the guy and chased him into the water—in December, in Halifax. Then he cast off with a storm brewing. Joe Russell summarized Lou's first voyage as a captain:

"It started with a desertion controlled only by police, and the threatened use of firearms. Then the mizzen boom lift parted, followed by the parting of the outer jib. Then the flying jib ripped to shreds, and the mizzen tore from chafing. The deserter successfully deserted, and (the vessel) returned to Nova Scotia with non-revenue-producing ballast. *Abundance* was nearly lost on the beach at Falkner's Island.

"It might be difficult," Russell concluded, "for anyone at the time to recognize this trip as the beginning of a legendary maritime career. Objective observers would probably consider it a disaster at sea. But Lou Kenedy was elated at his 'successful' voyage, and was as convinced he had made the right career decision."

It went on like that. On the next voyage (same vessel), out of Barbados, the ship's rudder was broken by another storm. A gale turned into a hurricane. Rudderless, *Abundance* somehow dodged many coral heads. "Rolling and strain on the gear was terrific," Russell wrote. With a hurricane howling, the boat was blown onto the beach in Jamaica. When they abandoned ship with their gear, crewmen were attacked by a gang of robbers. Lou shot one of them in the leg. The arrival of the police forestalled a nasty fight. "The police were so pleased to get the gang in jail," Russell wrote, "that the leg shooting was overlooked."

It got worse. On the second trip on Lou's next schooner, a 164-footer named *Adams*, a storm off Turks and Caicos islands blew swarms of moths and then hundreds of pigeons onto the boat's decks, clobbering crewmen and making a slimy, feathery mess. Below, the cook was badly cut after falling on the shard of a broken bowl. In the midst of all hell breaking loose, Lou was able to stop the bleeding. They made port, and the cook was treated. On the return to Turks they got hammered again. North of

Bermuda the vessel encountered the first of nine straight days of gales. The hull started working. "It was nothing alarming at first," Russell wrote, "because the boat leaked more than most schooners." But it became alarming enough that on the tenth day, Lou and crew were rescued by a passing freighter from which they watched their schooner sink. If one were keeping score, Lou Kenedy was one for three.

Undeterred, in 1934 Lou bought a swift 115-foot schooner named *Sea Fox* that in one race in 1889 had beaten the former America's Cup defender, *Mayflower*. Broke, and against his better judgment, Lou took on a financial partner in order to purchase the boat. The partner's name was Frank Muzzio. When *Fox* was hauled out in City Island, New York, for a refit, Lou was threatened with legal action after painting its bottom himself, violating the yard's policy prohibiting work by owners. "I can't pay you," Lou told the yard manager. "If you want to scrape the goddamn paint off, go ahead."

That was a hiccup compared to the battle Lou got into after Muzzio discovered the lead ballast in *Sea Fox* was worth more than the vessel, prompting him to sell the boat for scrap. After acquiring the proper court documents, Muzzio put a deputy marshal aboard to make sure Lou wouldn't try anything. The deputy was no match for Lou, as Russell relates it, and as Lou Kenedy told it in a 270-page interview he had with the Fisheries Museum of the Atlantic in 1980, eleven years before he died. The museum is in Lunenberg, Nova Scotia.

Following pages: the swift Sea Fox *was the prize of Lou Kenedy's fleet. She beat America's Cup defender* Mayflower *in an 1889 race..*

Aware that Lou meant to steal *Sea Fox*, the marshal burst out of the cabin, where Lou had locked him, and pulled a gun on Lou, who called the man's bluff. The marshal put the gun away and picked up a lead-filled billy sap. "I hauled out my .45," Lou said in the interview, "which was a big frontier model, and I pulled the hammer back. She clicked and I said, 'You fuckin' pirate, I'll blow your bloody brains out,' and he saw those leads lookin' out of the chambers. Why, he laid down when I said lay down, and I reached down and took his eyeglasses and pitched them overboard, took his badge and put it in my pocket, and I kicked him the ribs and I said 'Now get runnin.'"

It made the *Stamford Advocate* newspaper. The story included *Sea Fox* having run aground on the mud flats as Lou attempted to escape. While Lou waited for high tide to refloat his boat, a crowd gathered that included law-enforcement officials, interested parties, the state police, and onlookers.

"I propped a shotgun against one mast," Lou Kenedy said in his museum interview, "and my high-powered rifle against the other. I had my two .45s strapped around my waist and I just walked up and down the deck while this constantly growing group of officials and cops and curious bystanders argued and talked with me and each other across twenty feet of mud." When one lawman attempted to come aboard, Lou reminded him the yacht was private property. "If you come to get me be sure of your rights," Lou told him, "because the first step over the rail you'll be a dead man."

Russell paints a curious picture of groups of officials heatedly arguing among themselves over what action should be taken. Darkness fell. No one noticed the dinghy with three men aboard stealthily approaching *Sea Fox*'s far side. It was Lou's crew. The tide flooded. The crew quickly hauled up the outer jib and backed it against just enough wind to pull the sleek vessel off the mud and send her slipping into the channel. "In a few minutes," Russell wrote, "*Sea Fox* was nothing but a vanishing ghost, silently heading out to Long Island Sound."

Sea Fox ended up in Barbados, where Lou and crew restored the yacht to her freighter configuration and hauled cargo around the islands. Muzzio's attempted extradition of Lou failed. While in Barbados, Lou fell in love with Patricia Greenidge, the daughter of a Scottish physician. Patricia had just returned to the island after attending school in Scotland. In 1953 and 1954, the *Saturday Evening Post* ran a four-part series on Lou Kenedy written by Richard Thruelsen. Only Winston Churchill had ever received such extensive coverage by the *Post*. In that series, Thruelsen quotes Lou Kenedy: "It was in 1936 that Pat and I met. About a year after I was down there, we started going together. Her family was not too keen for her to get mixed up with a seafaring man. They had the English-Colonial awareness of caste."

Thruelsen, who describes Ms. Greenidge as "an attractive and vivacious young lady of twenty, a society belle," quotes her about her first date with Lou: "We met at a rather stuffy party. I think Lou noticed me because I did a Highland fling in costume, by request. Lou got a friend of his to call up and make a date. They came along a night later in a little English car that Lou had rebuilt himself. The body was all covered with canvas which he'd sewed together with sail twine. It had no doors, I remember. We all went dancing, then went down to *Sea Fox* which was in the harbor, and swam off the schooner."

As Thruelsen points out, when Patricia Greenidge's family discovered that the first Kenedy to migrate to the New World had done so in 1812, and had launched a very successful publishing firm, "they realized the Kenedys were a clan that qualified as quality." In 1936, a wedding took place. Lou's grandmother presented him with a full and clear title to *Sea Fox* as a wedding gift, and the couple sailed off on a honeymoon doubling as a freighting trip to Antigua. Lou's priorities were always evident.

The next boat, *Wawaloam*, was twenty feet bigger than *Sea Fox*. Lou said he bought it to take advantage of increasing freight rates. Listening to Thruelsen's description of the "disreputable wreck" of a boat brings to mind the tattered remains of *Puritan* Patsy Kenedy and Bill Bolling would encounter thirty-three years later: "The twenty-year-old schooner had settled into the mudflats of the Delaware River for years, with rotten masts, shredded rigging, and a riddled deck which sported an assortment of weeds." Lou and three workers he picked up managed to redo the deck before winter closed in. Pat and their first child, Brian, born in 1937, moved aboard. Making *Wawaloam* "seaworthy" was done on a shoestring without power tools, and reads like a project one should not try at home.

With no engine, *Wawaloam* relied on her undersized sail plan. Her first cargo was coal that had been improperly loaded, causing the vessel's bow to be way down. *Wawaloam* was impossible to steer until the coal was reloaded, a three-day job for four men with shovels.

"The first brisk breeze cracked the rotten bowsprit,"

Thruelsen writes. "Spray and rain sifted through everything, requiring all hands to wear oilskins. In the galley,
Pat cooked in a barrage of popping fat as water poured in
rivulets through the deck above." An engine was added, but
it was too small to move the boat in anything but calm conditions. On a future trip, an overload of lumber took the
boat to the edge of stability. Luckily that voyage was blessed
with moderate conditions. "It was as though the nautical
fates had taken pity on a helpless quarry," Thruelsen wrote.

The boat's condition was too rough even for Lou, who
was known for parting with every nickel as though it were
his last. But business had been good. He took *Wawaloam*
to Metegan, a fishing community on the west end of Nova
Scotia known for its quality shipbuilders. The metal box
in which Lou and Pat had been sleeping was replaced by
a proper cabin. Leaky decking was caulked, a new engine
was installed, and the boat's overall condition was sub-
stantially improved.

But the series of misadventures went on. There were
little things, like the ship's chronometer breaking. It ap-
pears the vessel was habitually overloaded with cargo. The
weather was not always kind. As Lou Kenedy wrote of a
trip in 1940, "In the Gulf Stream we hove to for eight days
in a series of heavy weather gales and southeasters. When
we tried to start the diesel we found the self-starter had
been ruined by sea water."

Lou created a method for hand-cranking the
high-compression Gray Marine 6-71 diesel so ingenious
it ended up in a service bulletin distributed worldwide.
But when one contemplates the plight of being hove to in
a leaky, overloaded old schooner at the mercy of wind and

seas for eight days in the Gulf Stream, the misery of it taxes any sailor's imagination. As Thruelsen put it, "Pat Kenedy must have wondered, during some of these trips, what strange twist of natural selection had steered her from the probability of a leisured life as wife of a British-colonial planter or businessman to the role of helpmate of a Connecticut-Yankee skipper." But Pat hung in there, cooking at all hours, keeping the quarters as shipshape as possible, even raising children on board as they arrived.

Wawaloam's last voyage would be in the late summer of 1942. The war had made it financially worthwhile for Lou to augment his regular cargoes of lumber, newsprint, hardware, Christmas trees, and dynamite with items like fan belts for cars and other scarce retail goods—as well as the ever-present haul of rum when running to Nova Scotia. The prewar trips were both profitable and enjoyable, but the increasing element of risk finally caused Pat and the young Brian to move ashore.

Pat wanted their land base to be Barbados, where she had grown up, and where she had family. "Daddy said his freighting might never take him to Barbados," Patsy says, "but he'd often be in Nova Scotia picking up and delivering cargo. She had to agree. They bought the big house on the river in Conquerall Bank. My mother endured so much. I didn't realize it at the time. The woman got dragged out of Barbados and got stuck in Nova Scotia with ten feet of snow."

"Mother was incredible," Rosie adds. "She was beautiful, she worked so hard, and Daddy was never home, away at sea the whole time. Until she moved ashore she had to be the mate and cook on all the rickety vessels

Lou had. But love is something. He loved her and she loved him, not to say they both didn't have things on the outside. That would be normal I guess. They were apart

Above: *Patsy's childhood home in Conquerall Bank, Nova Scotia.*
Below: *Baby Patsy (with mom) gets the feel of the wheel.*

so much those things happen. His crews used to bury the rum, then they'd contact Mommy to dig it up. She had a hard time."

Regardless of where they went, sending Pat and Brian ashore turned out to be a smart decision. On a clear, calm August day in 1942, with a load of molasses, all Pat's personal furniture, and the treasured MG TA with a canvas body Lou had sewn together on board, *Wawaloam* had departed Barbados and was headed for Saint John's, Newfoundland, when the torpedo announced itself. The noise was like the Doppler effect of a speeding train going by at close range: soft at first, then louder and much louder to a concussion-like crescendo followed by a rapid diminuendo. A torpedo. The men knew. Frozen helplessly in place, they heard a sound of explosive death passing a foot or two under their ship.

"There was a terrific bang and a shell landed in the water ahead of the vessel," Lou said. "We weren't too surprised. The eight schooners that had preceded us along this passage had been sunk by subs. We had everything prepared for a getaway."

As Lou told it, he and his crew launched two lifeboats that had been loaded with bags of clothes, food, fishing lines, and navigation instruments. Seven men and Butch, the ship's German shepherd, were in the boats five minutes after the torpedo had passed, after the shot had landed. The crew bent to the oars, and were soon half a mile away from *Wawaloam*. The submarine, a small one, maneuvered over to them. It was Lou's good luck that the sub's commander was not interested in murdering a bunch of civilian sailors—the torpedo notwithstanding. More good luck: the commander also spoke some English. His first question to the men in the lifeboats: "You haff what you need?"

Lou's pithy encounter with the U-boat's commander would secure his fame. His response: "Flashlights."

The commander couldn't hear him, motioned him to come aboard. Drawing on Lou's Fisheries Museum interview, Joe Russell recounts their encounter:

Lou: "What are you going to do now?"

Commander: "Destroy your ship."

Lou: "She's not winning the war for anybody. It's how I earn a living. You could let her go."

Commander: "I cannot do zat. *C'est la guerre.*"

Lou: "How about giving us a tow?"

Commander (incredulous): "A tow? A tow to vere?"

Lou: "To Bermuda."

Commander: "Vee are not going to Bermuda."

Lou: "Well anywhere is better than here."

Lou recalls one of the officers present grabbing his crotch and saying, "*Er hat Messingtestikel!*" Lou asked what he had said that caused his fellow officers to laugh.

Commander: "Your balls are made of brass."

Lou and the crew watched as the U-boat sank *Wawaloam* with its deck gun. The commander made sure Lou and his mates had basic needs. Six harrowing days later, with food and water about to run out, crew and dog were picked up by a small coal steamer headed home to Ireland. Wrong way. When they encountered a British corvette bound for Argentia, Newfoundland, Lou insisted on a transfer. The story of *Wawaloam*'s fate at the hands of a German U-boat and Lou's chat with the commander—including the brass-balls quote—made the *New York Times*. At the hotel in Argentia, Pat was waiting. Lou wouldn't be seen for two days. Patsy Bolling is quite sure that was when she was conceived.

******

There's a photograph of Patsy when she was three years old that tells a story. She is pictured with her mother bathing in a puncheon (an eighty-gallon wooden cask) full of water on the deck of another of Lou's boats, a 170-foot schooner named *City of New York*. The boat had originally been built as a heavily planked sealer. Admiral Richard Byrd had bought it for his first Antarctic expedition.

Patsy's father was away a lot, working both schooner and crew hard. In 1945, *City* encountered forty-foot seas, and took a terrible thrashing resulting in two men being washed overboard and lost. From *City*'s log of August 26 and 27, 1947: "Eugene Augustine falls from the masthead to deck breaking stays'l bullrope on the way, unconscious for a while but no bones broken or cuts & apparently no internal injuries, but severe shock etc. Doc took him to hospital for rest & observation. Cook AWOL and no supper. Aug 27: Eugene improving OK, cook in jail for drunkenness. Paid his fine and returned to vessel at 10:30 am. Gordon S. had gonorrhea & syphilis & went to hospital on Thursday for circumcision & wages stopped till he returns for work, etc."

As Joe Russell comments in *The Last Schoonerman*, "Apart from the nonchalance of the foregoing log entry, the significance is that Lou was first and foremost concerned about the damage to the bull rope, then he deigned to mention the injuries to poor Eugene. Next he laments the lack of supper so he bails the cook out of jail. The bail was not a gift, but a loan against wages. God only knows what happened to Gordon S., but he didn't get paid a minute of sick leave."

Living aboard, Patsy (age 3) bathes in a puncheon with her mother.
Following pages: Lou Kenedy's 170-foot, 515-ton schooner, City
of New York.

Meanwhile, Patsy, her mother, and her brother, Brian, were carrying on at their home in Conquerall Bank, which fronted the picturesque LaHave River. As late as the 1930s the broad LaHave was providing a convenient route for square-riggers to bring their cargoes of lumber to meet the railroad in Bridgewater, fifteen miles from the river's entrance at Riverport. Conquerall Bank is ten miles up the river. The Kenedy property consisted of forty acres, land that would be cut in half when the government exercised eminent domain to build a road. "Daddy put a big anchor out front to stop them," Patsy says, "but he lost that battle."

Patsy was one of twelve kids who attended the local elementary school. She got her first dog when she was five, a husky. She remembers him towing her to kindergarten on a toboggan. "My teacher was Mrs. Falkenham. She told us if we learned to spell her name, and spell Conquerall Bank, we'd be able to get by anywhere in the world."

Patsy remembers herself as a troublesome student, "mostly agitating, not paying attention." Part of the problem was the damaged left eye she was born with. The significant amount of blindness in that eye, her difficulty seeing and reading, wasn't realized until she was six years old. The eye wasn't surgically fixed straight ahead to appear normal until she was eleven. "The kids teased me about it," she says, "but that didn't bother me."

The rugged Canadian winter was also a time for skiing and skating. The latter turned perilous one day when Patsy, at age five, found a weak spot and fell through the ice. "The best part," Patsy says, "was being in the warm bed afterward

Opposite page: Patsy through the years, including first communion when she was eight, and dwarfed by City of New York's *wheel at age three.*

with Mother and Daddy, him giving me sips of rum to help get my body warmed up. Daddy said he broke through the ice in a dinghy and grabbed me just as my eyes went under."

Her other near miss was being thrown out of the family car on the way to church one Easter Sunday when she was seven. The car at the time was a Jaguar Mark IV, a handsome, large sedan with so-called "suicide doors" that opened from the front. Patsy's mom, who was driving (Lou was away), told her the passenger door was ajar and asked her to shut it. Patsy opened the door to slam it shut, the wind caught it, and she was pulled out of the moving car. She was thrown over the guardrail, and rolled down a steep embankment to the water's edge. Her Easter finery took a beating, but Patsy survived with scrapes and bruises. "Every time I go by that spot I giggle to myself," she says.

City of New York would be anchored in front of the house when Lou was home. There were always plenty of small boats around. Early on Patsy learned to raise an oar, lash it in place, and hang a towel on it for a sail. "I sailed and went swimming off the dock. No one was looking after me. There were no restrictions. I never even knew what a life jacket was." On summer freighting trips, the family would move aboard *City* for a vacation. Of sorts. It meant cooking on board for Pat, managing the kids in a riskier environment, and keeping belowdecks organized. For the kids, work was involved from the time they could pick up a shovel. As Lou once told onlookers who were moved to express concern as they watched Brian and Patsy toiling away, "Around here when they drop the bottle they gotta grab a rope."

Joe Russell pointed out a slight inequity: "Lou's daughters were his princesses. They could do no wrong."

Patsy recalls being so favored by her father that it caused friction with her mother. As a young tyke, she would often find herself making the rounds of business and bars at her father's side. As a six-year-old, she collected bottles and cashed them in, saving the money for a wristwatch. "The bigger bottles were worth two cents more," Patsy says, the memory crystal clear after seventy-four years, "and the

Patsy (right) with little sister Gabrielle aboard their father's three-master Vema *in the early 1950s.*

store guy was cheating me, giving me the same for all of them. I got my daddy, who was down the street at the bar. He got that straightened out. Maybe he made up the difference, I don't know. But I walked away with the exact money I wanted out of those bottles."

Patsy went back to the tavern with her father, and was left at the bar while Lou had a backroom discussion with the boss. On the wall, she spotted a photograph of the *Thomas W. Lawson*, famous in the seafaring community as the only seven-masted schooner ever built. "The barman saw me looking at the picture," Patsy says, "and he says, Oh, little girl, if you can name all the masts on that boat I'll give you the photo. I just laid it off for him: fore, main, mizzen, middle, spanker, jigger, driver. Ah, he says, isn't that wonderful, I think that's what they are. But nothing was happening. Daddy comes back and says,

Photograph of the Thomas W. Lawson *Patsy won at age six by naming all seven masts. Collecting her prize required a little help from Lou.*

Let's go. And I say, No no no, we can't go, the man owes me that picture. He told me if I named the masts—and Daddy said, You did, right? And I said, Yeah. Daddy tells the barman he owes the little girl that picture. He says the boss man would have his head. Daddy goes into the back and gets the boss man. The boss comes back and says, You name them for me also. So I tell him, fore, main, mizzen, middle, spanker, jigger, driver, and he says, Very good, little girl, and I went home proudly with the picture under my arm. It hangs in my living room today."

Brian, on the other hand, was expected to be as tough as his father. As Joe Russell wrote, "He was treated as a man, as a seaman, early in life." When he was nine years old, his father made Brian sign Articles of Convention, a legal agreement between crewmen and shipowners authorized by the International Labour Organization. The Articles are a statement of the rights and obligations of both parties, including wages (Brian was paid fifty cents a week), the capacity in which the seaman is to be employed, the period of employment, the scale of provisions to be applied to the seaman (Brian got three meals), the voyages to be undertaken, and so on. At age eleven, Brian was expected to stand all normal watches, and sleep in the fo'c'sle.

While having one's young son sign Articles on a family-run vessel is on the extreme side, on all but luxury yachts it is common for all hands aboard boats, guests included, to pitch in. Patsy says her first job on *City of New York*, at age four or five, was bringing in the log, clearing the seaweed and reading it. She also helped the cook bring meat soaking in brine out of the bully-beef barrel on the poop deck and retrieve vegetables from the open-slatted bins. "He baked bread every day," Patsy says, "and I'd get to eat the heels with lots of butter and sugar." There was playtime too. Early on, Lou let his kids know that having fun was fine as long as the work got completed first. "Daddy would fill the dory on deck with water," Patsy says, "and we'd pretend we were surfing when the ship rolled."

Patsy recalls that one of the early trips took thirty-three days. It was a round trip from Nova Scotia to Inagua, a tiny salt-rich island in the Caribbean. "We were gone thirty-three days," Patsy recalls, "so long I forgot which side of the LaHave River our house was on." So long that school had started, causing Patsy to be held back in kindergarten. She would catch up.

Portrait of the Kenedy family at chart table of Vema *in 1953, from left: Patricia, Gabrielle, Lou, Patsy, and Brian.*

Loading and unloading cargo was the hardest work for the kids. If Lou was taking on coal or salt, Patsy and her brother would be stationed on either side of the hold, scraping up the spill and shoveling it below. "With the salt, even if you wore gloves your hands got pickled," Patsy says. "Everything swelled up. It was awful."

When they got a bit older, the two would work the

main boom used to haul heavy loads of cargo (often salt or coal) aboard. The crewman on the windlass would lower the boom into the hold. Once loaded, Brian would swing the boom by hand onto the dock (or vice versa if loading),

*Patsy (general maintenance), with brother Brian (mate) and father Lou (skipper), crewing on **Alpha** in 1955.*

where it would be dumped. Patsy would then pull the empty boom back to be reloaded. "I had to find something to grab with my other hand because I was so little it was tough to move it," she recalls. "Once I got it moving it was okay."

Patsy says she's never been convinced her father had a more strident attitude toward her brother. "Brian kept saying how hard Dad was on him. I didn't get it, because I was behind him doing the same thing. And I was seven years younger. They had their disagreements, but it was the same rules for me. One time Brian wanted to go off and play baseball with a group from the next town, and Dad said get the work done, then you can go. Brian said he wanted to go now. Dad said finish the work. Brian wasn't measuring up. He wasn't doing well in school."

Brian passed away in 2022 at age eighty-five. In a letter written to his sisters ten years before he died, Brian expressed his feelings about his father. "I certainly waited too long to tell my father how much I loved him and how all I ever really wanted was his approval and love," Brian wrote. "I think he went to his grave never approving of me or loving me as I wanted, but that is certainly no reason why I shouldn't have told him how I felt."

The kids were all treated equally when it came to the dentist. "We all had our teeth done," Patsy says, "the doctor grinding away till he hit your brain. Mommy and Daddy kept saying just put up with it for the poor souls in purgatory. They haven't decided if they are going to heaven or hell. You know you're going to heaven because you've taken a lot of pain here. It turned out Daddy refused to pay for Novocain. It cost six bucks extra, you know. When I was around sixteen and I finally found out there was medicine they could give you, holy shit, I was in pig heaven."

When Patsy was nine years old, Lou acquired his sixth schooner, a two-hundred-foot three-master named *Vema*. He'd had ten good years with *City of New York*, but the ship's age (she'd been launched in 1885) had attracted the attention of the maritime authorities. Their respone was to lower the Plimsoll mark on the hull, a mark designating the maximum allowable draft of a vessel fully loaded. That would have cost *City* one hundred tons of cargo. Lou had solved the problem by repainting the Plimsoll where it had been, then uncovering the new official Plimsoll when it was inspection time. As Lou said, "This just goes to show that there was always some way to get around things."

But the maritime unions were getting stronger, taking hold, and that was a tougher problem to solve. On one of *City of New York*'s last trips to Barbados, Lou had to allow stevedores load sugar and rum, and fumed when twenty men showed up to do the work of ten. The next day there was a near altercation when Lou refused to let union workers load another thousand cases of rum. The sight of a fully enraged, oversized crewman of Lou's caused a group of pugnacious stevedores to back down. Lou's hatred of the unions was summarized by his description in the Fisheries Museum interview of a dockside confrontation he'd had with a union leader over using stevedores:

Lou: "Who the fuck are you?"

Leader: "You don't know who I am?"

Lou: "Don't know, don't give a shit."

Leader: "If you don't cooperate here, you'll never be able to offload in New York, and that's a promise."

Lou: "A fuckin' promise?"

Leader: "I'm dead serious."

Lou: "Then it's a deal. You get the fuck off my dock and I'll never offload in New York."

Shortly thereafter (in 1952), Lou Kenedy sold *City of New York* and the union problems that went with it. At the same time (within two hours) he purchased *Vema*, the 202-foot three-master. Originally launched in 1923, by the time *Vema* fell into Lou's hands it had been used as a dormitory for students at Kings Point Marine Academy, then abandoned at Staten Island.

Patsy with Butch, the ship's puppy, during her first summer crewing aboard the 202-foot, 544-ton Vema, *in 1953.*

It was scheduled to be broken up and sold for scrap. But by the time Patsy, who was nine, moved on board for the summer, the vessel had been cleaned up and chartered to Columbia's Lamont Geological Observatory (now Lamont-Doherty Earth Observatory for the study of climate and earth sciences) for a research cruise to the Caribbean and Gulf of Mexico.

Patsy had two summers on *Vema*. The second summer, Lou was just master, having sold *Vema* to Columbia after the first trip. The thirty-five mission-bound scientists who moved aboard did not measure up to Lou's idea of proper shipboard behavior, or to his notion of respect for the sea

Lou Kenedy and his husky, Gotlik, aboard Vema. *Gotlik was poisoned by charterers who felt threatened by the dog.*

and its traditions. The aloof scientists weren't happy with Lou's aggressive commanding presence, or with the husky guard dog that had come with the boat and that Lou had made his. And they didn't like putting up with Lou's daughter using the deck of the large schooner as her racetrack.

"For my ninth birthday," Patsy says, "Father made me a go-kart. I'd go roaring down the deck with the scientists screaming at me to get out of the way. And we're pretty sure they poisoned the dog. I was a kid on that boat. I polished some brass, but I was getting locked in cupboards and being a shit-disturber around the deck, for sure."

Patsy remembers being shocked by the next boat her father acquired, mainly because it was so small. She'd grown up on 150- and 200-footers. *Alpha*, the new girl, was an 80-foot ketch. "We couldn't imagine going to sea in such a little boat," Patsy says. "I was scared! Would it sink? Would it roll over?"

Like Lou's other boats, *Alpha* was in tough shape when he found it. That seems to have been a prerequisite for purchasing boats that was passed on to Patsy and Bill. *Alpha* was afloat, but as Joe Russell noted, "She dripped rust, but the hull seemed sound. Her teak deck was a mess, the rigging was a total loss, but the Dorman diesel was in good condition as was the embarrassingly opulent interior. 'But,'" Lou is quoted, reinforcing his number one priority, "'she could be had for a song. I sang that song and I got her.'"

After the usual essential cleanup, Lou and *Alpha* would have their adventures as they began chartering summers around New England. Thanks to Lou's keen reading of the weather, and coming upon a convenient harbor of refuge, *Alpha* was one of the few sailing survivors of Hurricane Carol, whose 120-mile-per-hour winds ransacked New York and New England in August of 1954 to the tune of $4.2 billion. Then Lou took a contract with the US Navy for a research mission in the Caribbean. It was a rich contract, one that would pay off his remaining debt on *Alpha* and then some. It also meant he'd be away from Conquerall Bank for six months at a time, putting more pressure on Pat, who would be left alone with the newborn Rosie, who had almost died at birth, and Patsy, Gabrielle, and Brian.

Becoming pregnant with Rosie had been a surprise, one Pat didn't handle well. She was forty-one years old, and already had her hands full with three children and a large, isolated house in a harsh climate to manage by herself. To further complicate matters, Rosie was born with celiac disease, an immune reaction to gluten. Recognizable and treatable today, celiac was a medical work in progress in 1954, when Rosie was born. "She almost died in the first five days," Patsy says. "She couldn't hold milk down. Finally one doctor figured it out, and had a special pablum sent from Boston. Daddy wasn't around. Rosie was in the hospital for months."

During her mother's pregnancy, Patsy was sent to Catholic boarding school in Halifax: Sisters of the Sacred Heart. She was dismayed, and confused. "Why, I wanted to know. I always wanted to know why. Drove my mother crazy. They told me it was because Mommy was overloaded. Brian was away at school. I was nine. Gabrielle was five. Daddy was away a lot. Mommy was older now. Maybe having Gay at home was enough. And here she was having another child. Maybe she didn't want to have to drive me to school every day. And I was a little terror."

As Joe Russell summarized it, "Patricia withdrew from the family and entered a period of deep depression. Lou, not known for his sensitivity, or, for that matter, his tolerance of the illnesses of others, simply ignored the problems and kept chartering *Alpha* while Pat stayed in

Conquerall Bank and withdrew further into her own dark world . . . If Lou knew anything of his wife's psychological crisis, he did not show it."

At Sacred Heart Patsy remembers being lonely. "Daddy told the nuns if I got bored they should have me redo all the doorknobs.

"We wore uniforms, and it was the first time I had been subjected to rules that were both strict and adhered to. For me it had always been—rules? Fuck the rules. Not at Sacred Heart, where it was God this and God that. I still profess to be a Catholic. But I eased out of it. I've been in a few churches since. But I have no sins to confess. God? Oh yeah. Somebody is up there. God or whatever. I'm still a believer, I still try to be a good person, sort of. But I learned in later years the best thing my parents did for me was to put me in school at Sacred Heart, and later at Mount Saint Vincent. I believe the Mount made me a no-slacker. I learned to play tennis. It made me see the light. Otherwise I could have been out of control."

Doctors finally convinced Lou that signing his wife on as cook for the Navy's Caribbean expedition would provide the therapeutic relief she needed from the heavy responsibilities of Conquerall Bank. With Rosie stabilized, a nurse was found who would look after her and Gabrielle. Patsy could live with family friends. Pat agreed to go.

"I heard later they wanted to give Mommy electric shock," Rosie says today. "Daddy wouldn't let them. Instead he took her to sea. Same thing. But she did recover."

Eventually. The trip did little to alleviate Pat's depression. She did her duties, but she seldom spoke, and she kept to herself. She spent her off hours walking the beach of Isla de Aves (Bird Island), a tiny islet 150 miles southeast of Antigua where the Navy was conducting its research. Watching the gannets ravenously gobbling up the baby turtles that were hatching and crawling out of the sand was what triggered her psychotic episode, which lasted more than a month. Day after day Pat drove herself to exhaustion gathering turtles and putting them safely into the sea while screaming bloody murder and swinging sticks at the hovering predators.

She slept on the beach. Every couple days she went to the boat to clean up and eat something. One of the scientists aboard was finally able to break through Lou's resistance and at least make him accept his wife's obsessive behavior. He took her some blankets. Then one day it was over. Pat returned to *Alpha*, ready to resume cooking. When the charter was finished, Pat flew back to Nova Scotia and her children. Lou chartered *Alpha* to a movie company making *Flame of the Islands*.

Lou had been hatching a plan. He'd realized his business hauling cargo under sail was coming to an end. He wanted to leave the house at Conquerall Bank and move the family to the Bahamas, where he would charter around the islands. It was a tough sell. Unlike Lou, Pat had established a life for herself in Nova Scotia. She had friends, activities, commitments. And her mental state was still on the fragile side.

"It was a tough job being married to Lou," Patsy says today. "I'm so sorry I didn't know more about my mother. We were always at odds. But can you imagine if you're an island girl being married to this adventure man who was sailing off everywhere, and there was the war, and living in the wilds of Nova Scotia, and having to raise four kids pretty much by herself, and now he wants to move to the Bahamas?"

Lou backed down. He got ready for another charter season in New England waters. This time Patsy stepped up and asked to go—having determined that the little eighty-footer probably wouldn't roll over. "I took her," Lou said, "because it was good company for me and she was a great girl to be with and she was very attentive and would listen and learn anything about ships that was possible."

Patsy says her summer on *Alpha* was when she came into her own. "I was bosun when I was eleven. We were chartering out of Essex, Connecticut. I polished the brass and did the laundry, changing the sheets after every charter." She only ran afoul of her father once, when she skirted the "work comes first" rule. She wanted to go to Coney Island with some of the crew on an off day, but she had laundry to do. She knew if she did separate loads, she'd miss the trip. She washed the blue towels with the white sheets. The result: blue sheets. "I got in such trouble. I brought them all folded back to the boat, hid them, and went to Coney Island. Daddy was furious. He had to buy new sheets."

A hardworking summer afloat would not appeal to many eleven-year-old girls, but Patsy loved it. "It was special for me because I was with Dad. I often wondered why Mommy let me go. She wasn't fond of me hanging around with him." One incident in particular had infuriated her mother. Patsy had gone to Bridgewater with her father one day when she was eight or nine. He'd stopped for a haircut. When the barber finished, Lou told him he might as well cut his kid's hair. The boyish cut completed Patsy's skinny, tomboy look, causing her mother to burst into angry tears. "I didn't mind," Patsy says, "but Mommy was very upset.

"I figured letting me go on *Alpha* was Mommy's way of making Daddy be true-blue, not drink too much, not womanize—whatever—because his daughter was along. And I think my presence did keep him in line. In Essex there was always a beach party on Friday nights. People came with hamburgers and hot dogs, but I would bring fish for us. Dad would look at me—Are you kidding?—but we'd eat the fish because we were Catholics.

"He liked having me along. I could flake and furl the jib on the bowsprit. I got to drink ten percent of every bottle of beer my father opened. It started by how much I could guzzle. Then he had to put a limit on it. By the end of the summer I could almost drink a whole bottle in one gulp. I was learning quickly. I had lots of good training." She had also picked up Lou's habitual cursing, a vernacular that would stay with her.

Patsy's highlight of the *Alpha* summer was when her father put her in charge of the boat's eighteen-foot lapstrake launch. "I was captain of that boat. It was my introduction to engines. It had a little Stuart Turner single-cylinder two-stroke engine I had to keep serviced and running. I was in charge. It was my boat. I got the gas and changed the oil, cleaned the spark plug and the fuel filter, wiped down the varnish every morning, got the groceries, and ferried the charterers back and forth. Polishing brass was not something I wanted to do all my life, but I learned if I put Vaseline on the brass it would stay looking good for four or five days."

The Kenedys just prior to casting off for Nassau in 1955.
From left: Patsy, Patricia, Rosie, Lou, and Gabrielle.

III

NASSAU

As usual, Lou's wishes would prevail. His argument that the business of carrying freight under sail was no longer profitable carried the day. The family would be uprooted from Nova Scotia and sailed (how else?) to Nassau. The move was painful for his family, from selling the house and having to bid farewell to dear friends to the thankless task of narrowing one's possessions down to what would fit on an eighty-foot sailboat carrying three youngsters and two adults. Brian was absent, having joined the Navy before the family departed for Nassau. The fourth night out on *Alpha*, one of the worst possibilities afloat occurred: one of the crew went missing. It was Rosie, who was not quite two years old at the time.

"It's my earliest memory," Rosie says today from her home in Jupiter, Florida, where she lives with three cats and two dogs. "When I got lost. They had put me in the wheelhouse. I remember lying down up there and getting really cold. I was so uncomfortable. I wasn't supposed to leave the wheelhouse. But I went down and curled up in the life jackets that were stored under the settee. I went to sleep nice and warm. I woke up and heard there was an issue going on. I was so young, but I do remember thinking maybe I ought to come out. I came out . . . Are you looking for me, hey?"

It was Pat who was almost lost that night. The thought of her child going over the side put her in shock. It was October, 2:00 a.m., cold at sea. *Alpha* was motor-sailing 350 miles off the coast of New Jersey on course for Nassau. It was a very dark night. No moon. No lights of other vessels to be seen. The seaway was bouncy. Sailing at night on the ocean is so solitary. A boat's speed seems to increase in the dark. The figures around the helm become blurry shadows in the glow of the red binnacle light. If you've never been at sea, with nothing but water to the horizon in every direction, on a tiny speck of a vessel on a windswept, dark, undulating desert of ocean, it is sobering. Humbling.

Sobbing, emotions shattered, on her knees Pat beseeched her husband to turn back and begin searching for their child. Lou knew how impossible that would be in mid-ocean, at night. Rosie could have gone over hours before her absence was discovered. Finding the proverbial needle in the haystack would have been simple by comparison. Lou knew, and refused to budge. "I'm not going back," he said in his captain's voice. "If she's over, she's gone." It was about then they heard the little voice: "You looking for me, hey?"

Patsy got the worst of it. Much as it upset her big sister, Rosie had been made her responsibility. Because she was eleven years older than her new baby sister, the job of in-house sitter had fallen into her resentful lap. "To have that responsibility at that age," Patsy says, "that's where Mom and I almost came to blows. We were always having arguments. When I would get home from school in Nassau, Rosie wasn't even going to school yet. When she was two, three, four, five, I had to care for her. I'm thirteen, fourteen, wanting to go sailing, there's Rosie. I'm playing tennis, there's Rosie sitting over there. When I was really mad and wanted to do something on my own, I'd flush a diaper down the toilet. Plug it up. All hell would break loose, had to call the plumber, everyone running around, and I'd think with all these people they can take care of Rosie, and I'd split. I think that's why I never wanted to have kids. Bill had two, first of all. And I'd taken care of Rosie for so many years I knew I didn't want kids. I'd had enough. I knew it was something I didn't want to do.

"For the rest of that trip on *Alpha*," Patsy says, "Daddy made me tie a string connecting Rosie's and my big toes at night.

"It was about then I actually had some goals. Never had any since," she says with a smile, "but when I was twelve my goals were to get rid of Rosie, and sail around the world in a Friendship sloop. I was too dumb to know you couldn't sail around the world in a Friendship sloop. Back then I also didn't know you could go transatlantic in a 12-meter."

Later in life Patsy realized she did have one, overriding goal, one that she actively pursued: adventure.

******

Alpha arrived in Nassau, Bahamas, in late October 1955. Pat Kenedy had undergone the trial of moving from a warm island life to the freezing temperatures, driven snow, and isolation of a Nova Scotian village where being an outsider was a lonely condition. Thirteen years later, it was back to what northerners often mistake for paradise. "To us," Patsy says, "Nassau was just another island. We'd seen plenty of Caribbean islands on summer family cargo trips with Daddy. And Mommy had been raised on Barbados, after all. Nassau was beautiful, true. The climate, the great beaches and color of the water. But my sisters and I, Mommy too, we were all mad at Daddy for moving us. I was yanked out of my comfort zone when I was eleven. We had to leave our friends, our lives. He gave away my dog, my toboggan, snow skis. I wasn't happy. But you didn't say anything. You just did what you had to do."

Money was tight at first. The Kenedys lived on the boat for several weeks before they found a small rental one block from Nassau Harbour—two bedrooms and one bath for parents, three kids, and a cat (Brian, remember, had joined the Navy). Patsy and Gabrielle were immediately entered in Xavier's College, Sisters of Charity. They rode the six miles to school every day on a tandem bicycle given to them by Lou's brother during a stop they'd made in City Island, New York. "I drove," Patsy says, "that's why they called me Bossy Boots. Chatty Kathy was in the back, not pedaling too much."

There were lots of lessons to be had. The school offered piano, but Patsy didn't take to the piano. She was told
she had to play some instrument. Her choice was accordion. What she had meant was a little squeeze-box. What

her mother got her was a full-size accordion. "I hated that
fucking accordion," Patsy says today. "But I had made the
decision, so I had to eat it. After a year or so Gay and I had
gotten our own bikes. For my lesson I had to ride my ass
over the hill in Nassau, quite a big hill, with the accordi-

on hanging off my handlebars. With it hanging there you could only go straight, not make any turns. Not fun."

The dancing lessons were tolerable, but the tennis lessons with Frank Budge (brother of Don Budge, the

first American to win the Grand Slam), and water-skiing lessons with Bruce Parker (the first USA water-skiing champion) were great fun. It was the acquisition of a little Bahamian sloop that made Patsy's life complete. She called it *Tipky*—short for *This Is Patsy Kenedy's Yacht*. Her father had started the naming tradition when he was a boy, calling his first boat *Tilky* (*This Is Lou Kenedy's Yacht*). "I was in pig heaven," Patsy says, "when I got my sailboat." She also had to learn to keep the boat's cranky British two-stroke Seagull outboard engine running, a challenge all Seagull owners will understand. It's no wonder Rosie

turned out to be a good sailor. She had plenty of early instruction at Patsy's hands.

Patsy started racing go-karts when she was fifteen. The kids raced karts powered by little Briggs & Stratton engines at Oakes Field, the local airport. They set courses with cones, and held scavenger hunts. Patsy discovered she had a flair for driving, and she liked it. It became a satisfying outlet for her competitive needs. Jim Jensen, a fellow driver from those days, remembers her well even after six decades. "She always upped the ante," Jensen says. "She pushed you, and she could handle those karts. A lot of the kids drove to screw around and have fun. When Patsy was on the course, you'd better pay more attention. She was out to whip your butt."

Patsy participating in a Bahamas Development Board promotion aboard Tipky. *"I could play a couple songs," she says.*

With the children getting older, and with Patsy taking care of Rosie much of the time, Pat Kenedy jumped into is-land life. She took a job at the British Colonial hotel running the beach shop, renting towels and chairs, selling sandwiches and cold drinks. She wanted extra money for her children, who were the best-dressed girls in Nassau town. Having her mom in charge also made it easy for Patsy to sail *Tipky* off the hotel beach. She took tourists sailing for a small fee.

Meanwhile Lou was off chartering to groups, making one- and two-week trips down islands. Business was good, except for summers because of the heat. It didn't help matters that *Alpha* was not only not air-conditioned, but it had

Babysitting was a chore for Patsy, but sister Rosie had fun

a coal-fired Aga cookstove that had to be kept burning. The Aga provided comfort on chilly nights, but in summer, the boat was a steam box below. No problem for the intrepid Kenedy family—including Brian, when on leave from the Navy—who would sail off together to various islands in

August for diving, sailing, and exploring until it was time for school to start. Air-conditioning wasn't omnipresent at the time, and there were still some islands left to explore.

Just as she had been able to select what musical instrument to learn, Patsy got to pick her boarding school when she was fifteen. It was an easy choice. By going back to Nova Scotia, she could reunite with her old pals. Several of them planned to attend Mount Saint Vincent University, an all-girls Catholic school in Halifax. Patsy chose to join them.

Those who have known Patsy over the years comment on her having what they call "an eye for the job." In short, the expression describes one's ability to see a job, like a sail in need of trimming or a dish that needs washing, and get it done before anyone else even sees it. Like hand-eye coordination, having an eye for the job is innate. Even if you only have one good eye.

For Patsy, the tendency to see jobs got fine-tuned sailing with her father, with whom such prescient behavior got points. "Maybe I got it from Lou," Patsy says. "He never left anything a mess or awry. Sails were always perfectly trimmed, lines were coiled." She says it might also have come from her competitive side: "Got to get it done before someone else. At the Mount, on Saturdays we had to change our sheets and polish our floors. I'd be up at six, be the first one to get the floor-polishing machine. Had breakfast at seven, then had the morning to do what I wanted. The rest of the kids slept in and ended up fighting over the machine."

Patsy's nature to test the rules was kept busy at the Mount because there were plenty of them enforced by

Following pages: The Mount St. Vincent Academy class of 1961. Patsy is seated, far left.

the nuns who ran the place. Patsy thought nothing of sneaking out of her dorm at night, using the elevator (off-limits to students), and going to the kitchen for a glass of milk and a cookie. "The Canadian girls weren't into that sort of thing," Patsy says. "When Canadians are told not to do something, they don't do it. The girls worried I'd get into trouble. I did, finally. Friends came to visit. They were smoking, and gave me a puff. The nuns said I was smoking. I said, No, it was just a puff. The more I protested, the more weeks they added on. I was campused for six weeks. Dad complained. Why can't she come home for Easter? Because she's grounded. He said, Won't that sour her? The head nun told him: You run your ship, I'll run my school."

During Christmas, on her first vacation back home in Nassau, Patsy met Ted Turner for the first time. Turner's future sailing exploits—winning the America's Cup and being selected four times as US Sailing's Rolex Yachtsman of the Year—would be exceeded only by his success as a media and professional sports mogul that would make him a billionaire by age fifty (see these books: *The Grand Gesture: Ted Turner, Mariner, and the America's Cup* and *Ted Turner: The Man behind the Mouth*, by yours truly). Ten years after their first meeting, Patsy would have a hand in helping Turner win the World Ocean Racing Championship. But their first meeting was happenstance.

Turner's family had chartered a large sailboat for the Christmas holidays. The boat happened to be moored at the same dock in Nassau as *Alpha*, making it likely that Patsy and Turner would meet. Ted was nineteen or twenty, Patsy fourteen or fifteen. She doesn't remember. "Let's go with fifteen," she says. "That will take some of the edge off me driving, drinking, and dating a twenty-year-old."

They met on the dock. Patsy liked Turner's looks, his inquiring eyes, the deep dimple on his chin. Ted was known for his appreciation of female charms, and at fifteen, Patsy was awash in them. She had left her tomboy self behind. Of course they stopped to talk.

"One of the first things Ted said to me," Patsy recalls, "was: Are you a virgin? He wanted to know what was happening around town. I said, Junkanoo starts tomorrow morning. If you wanna go I can pick you up at four a.m. He said fine, so at four a.m. there he was. I picked him up on Daddy's scooter."

They went to the Prince George Hotel, where a friend of Patsy's had rented a room with a balcony overlooking the Bay Street parade route. The booze was flowing as the sun came up. The parade started at 6:00 a.m., ended at 8:00.

"Ted bought some drinks, I bought some drinks," Patsy says. "When it was over, he suggested we have breakfast. We went to some joint for eggs and grits. He paid. He wrote his address in my book, which I still have. It says, 'Teddy Turner.'"

******

Patsy graduated from Mount Saint Vincent with honors. She was awarded a gold medal for the highest aggregate in the commercial class she had taken to obtain employment tools (shorthand, typing). But not before she exercised her theory that laws were made to broken. It had to do with the curved marble double staircase in the main building of Mount Saint Vincent, a magazine-quality staircase that was strictly off-limits to students. It happened as the administrators prepared for the annual senior prom.

"They brought all us senior girls in," Patsy says, "to explain how the prom worked, where food would be and all that. I stuck my hand up and said, I'll have my prom dress on, and I want to walk down that marble staircase. They said, You can't come down those stairs. I'm sure I had walked up and down them one night just to say I'd done it, but I said, We've been here all these years and that's the least you can do is let us walk down those marble stairs, how wonderful, with our dates waiting at the bottom to give us a flower. Maybe

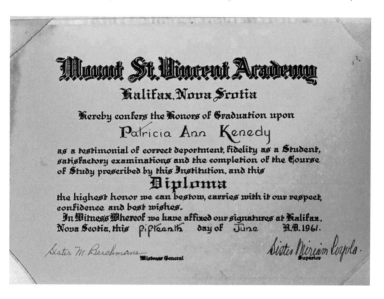

one person stood behind me. The rest were thinking, Good idea, but no one dared speak up about it. I said, Hey, you're getting rid of us, give us that last walk down the marble stairs and out the door. And they did."

Patsy's graduation made the Personally Speaking column of the *Nassau Guardian* newspaper: "Proud parents this week are the Lou Kenedys who attended the graduation of their eldest daughter, Patsy, at her school in Nova Scotia . . . When she returns home on Tuesday she will find Daddy's Jaguar (1951 XK 120) all splendidly polished and registered in her name awaiting her at the

airport." The *Guardian* neglected to report that Patsy had also been given a Siamese cat named Suzie Wong.

The Jag wouldn't stay polished for long. It would catch fire on turn four of Patsy's first significant automobile race.

******

Patsy put her typing and shorthand to work as a secretary at the Nassau Harbour Club, which was under construction, but her eye was on the racetrack at Oakes Field, where she'd been karting for several years. During the war, the Royal Air Force had two airbases in Nassau: Windsor and Oakes Field. Car racing started at Windsor in 1954, moved to Oakes in 1958.

In those days, kids in Nassau started driving when they were young teenagers. Those with the need for speed, like Patsy, were racing by the time they were sixteen. She started in Austin-Healy Sprites and Morris Minis loaned to her by fellow members of the Bahamas Automobile Club. "I was seventeen, eighteen," she says. "I just wanted to see if I could do it. I never had any lessons. Safety? I put this leather thing on my head, got a jumpsuit, came off the street, and started racing."

They used standing starts based on lap times, with the beginners in the back. Patsy quickly worked her way to the front, as photos from those days attest. After graduation, she had announced to her parents she'd be leaving for America in a couple weeks to find her way in the world. "But I came home," she says, "to find a studio apartment my mother had furnished for me, with the rent paid; a job I really liked; and the XK 120 Daddy gave me. Why would I want to leave?"

The call of the Jaguar sitting out front of her apartment was too much to resist. And the eighth annual Bahamas Speed Week (1961) was coming up, an event that had taken off since it began in 1954, attracting winning drivers like Masten Gregory, Phil Hill (2), Lance Reventlow, Dan Gurney (2), and Stirling Moss (2). Her father had raced the Jaguar in Speed Week in the mid-1950s, so he was all for Patsy taking part.

"Speed Week!" Patsy says. "Importing all these good-looking men from all over the world! I had to figure out how to be a part of that. I belonged to the auto club. I volunteered to put posters up all over town and do whatever they needed. I figured I'd take the Jag, go round the course, get free gas and a set of tires, and have some fun."

Bahamas Speed Week had a ladies' race on the program. Patsy says that in her entire racing career she never encountered another ladies' race until much later. "Back then, in the '60s," she says, "the men were not only accepting of us but happy to loan us cars, and were always there to help us with mechanical problems and other stuff we needed." I'll bet. Having a car loaned to you—to race!—seems like a fairly large loan. But men being men, and Patsy being not only an attractive, shapely blonde, but one who could maybe leave them behind on the track, talk engines, and handle her rum afterward, produced that level of trust.

Patsy was in fact having fun until turn four of the ladies' race. A battery cable shorted out and ignited the canvas top stuffed behind the seats. A *Nassau Guardian* article on the race, which included news about the difficulty of getting parts delivered for Stirling Moss's featherweight Lotus, was one-upped by a large photograph of Patsy's Jaguar being consumed by flames. The caption reads: "Jaguar roadster driven by Patsy Kenedy burns after Patsy steered the car off the Oakes Field course Saturday and hopped out when it burst into flames."

Race organizers could only grit their teeth as the race was delayed more than two hours while the fire trucks responded to the burning car, and then to the bushes that had caught fire, and while the smoldering car was being dragged off the track. But the unfortunate accident was turned into a lighthearted moment among the four hundred attending the closing Motor Ball at the Montagu Beach Hotel when Patsy, fetching in a long, strapless dress, accepted the Hard Luck trophy with a laugh and an engaging smile. Presenting the trophy was His Excellency Robert de Stapledon, KCMG, governor of the Bahamas. The following day, the *Guardian*'s

Opposite page: *Speed Week 1961, Patsy was running third in her Jaguar until it caught fire.* **Above:** *She received the Hard Luck trophy.*

race coverage featured a photograph of Patsy dancing with Stirling Moss. Dates, after that, were not hard to come by.

Having a burnout on one's first race would have intimidated many novice drivers, perhaps moving them on to a less combustible form of competition. For Patsy—with her one good eye, don't forget—it meant finding another car in time for the following year's Speed Week and the arrival of more dashing men. She borrowed some money from Lou, who kept careful notes of such transactions in a small black book, and bought a Porsche 356B Carrera.

******

While Patsy was becoming familiar with her new car in preparation for the next Speed Week, the man who would become her partner was nearly removed from that pleasure. Bill Bolling and his current wife, Betty Miller, were in the back seat of a friend's car, returning to their home in Rye, New York, after attending a play in Manhattan. Their car was broadsided. Betty suffered a broken elbow, a broken arm, and several broken fingers. Bill bore the worst of it, including a concussion and severe facial damage.

Bill was repaired, and he healed very well thanks to excellent surgery. Bad headaches were the only residual. The doctor told him that if he got a manual sewing machine and made some things, it would help with the headaches. He made a set of nautical signal flags. As often happens after a brush with death, Bill used those long, uncomfortable weeks of rehabilitation to take stock of his life.

He had been born into a First Family of Virginia whose heritage could be traced back to that famed Native American, Princess Pocahontas of the Powhatan people—by all accounts (British Colonialists' and Walt Disney's standards included) an attractive woman. She would be featured by the Jamestown Settlement to promote immigration from the UK. Pocahontas had married a Colonist and had borne a child who in turn produced a grandchild named John Bolling. Two hundred fifty years later, John Bolling's descendant, Bill, found himself in a bit of a rut, commuting to work at his father's advertising agency and a partner in a failed marriage with two children.

Life had started strangely for Bill Bolling. He was six months old when his parents divorced, an event that sent his father packing. One evening when he was twenty years old, enjoying a few drinks in a bar in Los Angeles, a man had approached Bill asking if he were George William Bolling III. He said he was. The man then introduced himself as George William Bolling II—his father. GWB II was a frequent traveler to California, where he had established a branch of his advertising business.

After a successful familiarization period, GWB II suggested his son run the California company. Bill went to New York for training, then moved back to California. In 1959, GWB II closed the Los Angeles office. Bill and his family moved back East, where he was commuting to Manhattan every day. Now he was thirty-five years old. He realized he was bored. Having been spared on the highway, he vowed to make the most of his second chance.

With divorce approaching, Bill decided to take a break, make some changes. He chose Florida, a likely destination for an ambitious East Coast yachtsman. He would take with him only the essentials: his pink forty-foot Alden yawl named *Yahoo*; his pink 1957 Chevy Corvette, and Eggemoggin, his Siamese cat who was named after a lovely body of water in Maine. He would accomplish this by sailing *Yahoo* 150 miles or so down the Intracoastal Waterway, then hitchhiking back to the car. He would then drive three hundred miles south and hitchhike back to the boat, where Eggemoggin was waiting. And so on, until he got to Florida. It worked out just fine. Each day he would put a bag of ice under his Panama hat to temper the pain of the headaches, and set off.

He ended up berthing *Yahoo* at Bahia Mar, a lively yachting center in Fort Lauderdale. "It was playtime for him," Patsy says, "living on his boat at Bahia Mar, having a gay old time that included fun visitors like the Mamas and the Papas." Bill had very little money left by the time he got to Florida. The paychecks from the Bolling Company had stopped. He took day work at the marina, which led to diving jobs and then deliveries for local yacht brokers. Any thoughts of returning to Rye, New York, dimmed. As the possibilities of making a life on the water became more and more attractive, and realistic, messages from his father inquiring about his return to work were put aside.

"Bill was fired from the Bolling Company six months later," Patsy says. "He would never see his father or speak with him again." Ten years later, in 1972, he'd receive a letter from a lawyer stating that GWB II had died, and that GWB III was excluded from any inheritance.

******

Patsy took her racing up a notch in the 1962 Speed Week, placing fifth out of twenty-three Formula Vee cars in the Locals first heat and sixth out of twenty-one cars in the second heat. Patsy was the only female driver in the Locals category. In the ladies' race she was third (out of seven cars) in both heats. Average speeds were in the eighty-mile-per-hour range.

She recalls the men drivers being totally welcoming to her presence on the track. And helpful. For one reason, she was full of questions for them, about everything from driving techniques to mechanical issues, questions she always

Following pages: *Patsy rolling a tire into the garage for her Porsche (n16), then happily awaiting the start.*

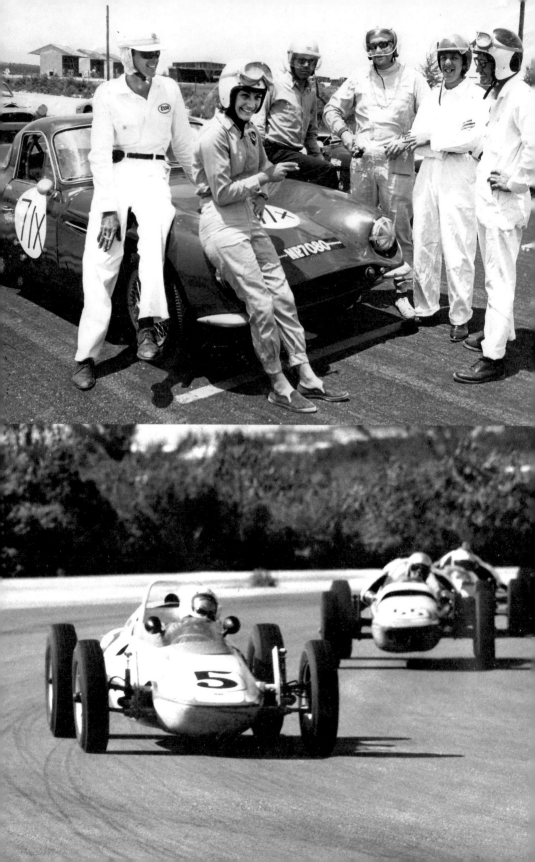

Opposite page: *Patsy with fellow Bahamas Auto Club drivers (top), and leading in a Formula Vee race (bottom) during Bahamas Speed week.* **Above:** *Patsy with trophy for winning the Ladies Race.*

presented in that straightforward, slightly disarming way of hers, with irresistible eye contact. Disarming because they were good questions, based on her experience. She'd been fooling with engines and driving since she was eleven.

If that weren't enough, all another driver had to do was look at the attractive figure over there with her fire suit pulled down around her hips, her head bent into the engine compartment of the Porsche, focused on changing engines after racing was finished. The Porsche was her everyday ride as well as her race car. She used a Volkswagen engine for getting around Nassau.

"I had help the first several times," she admits. "I finally got the change down to about four hours." On her own, without asking for help. The perky blonde asked for no quarter, a way of participating that made her accepted and even admired by the men, many of whom weren't up to changing an engine. Her obvious ability, her friendly disposition, her sporting approach on the track, and her eye-pleasing self completed a dynamic package.

Perhaps most importantly, Patsy likes men. "It wasn't about getting laid," Patsy says. "I came late to that. I just happen to like men. I prefer their company." Today she belongs to a group of friends that meet for dinner on Tuesdays. Several of them often meet for a drink at a nearby tavern before dinner. "I'll walk in and see two tables, one of women, one of men. I'll go to the men's table every time."

If a woman likes men, chances are the men will respond in kind. Men need all the female friends they can get.

Patsy's indulgence of her femininity by using a black Magic Marker to turn her car's headlights into lashed eyes drew no smirking from the other drivers. If they had known the significance of the eye on the left headlight, which was winked shut, they would have been even more impressed. Patsy says having one bad eye never bothered her. "I had to jump through hoops to race cars. They said I had to have an outside mirror. As for flying, the instructor took me through the paces, said if I could do it I was fine. I don't seem disabled by it. It was never a deterrent or

a worry except for my eye doctor, who was astounded I would be doing things that could damage my good eye."

She kept driving in local races at Oakes Field throughout the year, but her focus was on the Speed Weeks, where she consistently finished in the top three while competing against both men and women. In 1963 she won top points in her class driving a Porsche 356B. In 1966 the fire trucks were called out again, this time to help a rival lady driver who was competing with Patsy in a one-lap race to break a tie for first overall. "I passed her and then heard the bang," Patsy told the *Nassau Guardian*. "I looked in my rearview mirror and there she was off the track against a tree."

In a later ladies' race, when a competitor's car caught fire, Patsy slammed to a stop to make sure the driver got out safely. Dennise McCluggage, another accomplished woman driver of the time, roared past to take the checkered flag. The judges awarded the win to Patsy, who had been running a solid first when she had stopped.

Herbert Fishel pioneered the emphasis on driver safety during his twelve-year tenure as executive director of General Motors Racing (Fishel retired in 2003). He says the institution of driver safety took a long time, not really coming together until the 1990s. "Patsy represents an era I was aware of," Fishel says, "but until I met her I never talked with someone who had lived through it. It was a dangerous era, a raw sport—leather helmets, T-shirts—with drivers fully exposed to the elements. Lots of folks died. Patsy and other drivers like Stirling Moss, Roger Penske, Jim Hall, the Rodriguez brothers, and Carroll Shelby knew the risk, accepted it, planned for it, and persisted. That exposure helped make Patsy a confident, self-assured lady.

"She wasn't fazed by those prominent drivers," Fishel says, "like Moss, who was the hero of that era. She took it all in, used the notoriety of these people in a positive way. She didn't put on any airs. She remained her inimitable Patsy self. I know she once took one of the Rodriguez brothers from the hotel to the track on the back of her scooter."

******

Patsy lost her Harbour Club job after a confrontation with her boss. Toward the end of one shift, he wanted her to work late. She had plans she didn't want to cancel. He said either work late or quit. She quit. "My parents were distressed. Maybe I was too big for my boots."

A few days later she was water-skiing, and stopped at the beach on Hog Island. Hog had been recently purchased by A&P supermarket magnate, Huntington Hartford, who would rename it Paradise Island. He was planning a resort worthy of its grand name. "I met some employees," Patsy says. "They said they were looking for water-ski instructors, so I signed on."

Patsy became part of the island's water-ski shows, with pyramid formations and jumps performed on the ocean side of the island, often in three-foot waves. There was a bar with tables on the beach where customers could watch the shows, which were done at night, with spotlights, while having a drink and scrunching their feet in the sand. "I was the clown," Patsy says, "riding in a chair with skis fastened to its legs."

One of her fellow skiers was Jimmy Lowe, who had a water-sports concession at three of Nassau's beach hotels. Jimmy also drove in local races at Oakes Field. As young teens the two had competed in karts. "The bridge to Paradise Island was open," Lowe says. "I had a Jaguar. Patsy had a Porsche. Sometimes we'd meet at the foot of the bridge and race over the bridge to Paradise Beach. There was very little traffic in those days. And the road to Paradise Beach was pretty good. Paved. Patsy was a good driver, saw herself as one of the guys so to speak. Very attractive, and gifted. I was four years younger, so I never made a pass at her."

At the same time Patsy was teaching sailing in ten-foot O'Day Sprites. George Damianos, who has been in the real estate business in Nassau for fifty-some years, was barely ten years old at the time, but he remembers her. "She kept track of us," he says, "making sure we didn't drown or sail off into the blue."

Damianos also remembers Pat Kenedy, who was very supportive of the sailing program for kids. Pat often picked up a car full on Saturday mornings. "One day a group of us were watching cartoons," George says, "and we were disorderly. We got expelled for two weeks for being rude. Pat organized a trip for us on her husband's boat to tiny Hawksbill Cay in the Exumas. We slept on deck. Patsy and her sister Gabrielle were on board. They played a trick on us, telling us we could go to the movie theater there. We scrambled for shoes and money, and just before we were to get in the skiff they said there was no theater. I played the same trick on my children years later, took them to the Exumas and said there was a pizza parlor down there."

Another one of Patsy's students was Craig Symonette, son of Sir Roland, the first prime minister of the Bahamas after self-government in 1964. Craig, an entrepreneur who founded Bahamas Ferries, would go on to be one of the Bahamas' most successful international sailors. He and his older brother Bobby represented the Bahamas in the 1972 Olympics (Soling) with a third crew, Percy Knowles. The Symonettes were podium regulars in the elegant 5.5-meter class for many years.

"The Sprites we sailed with Patsy were little hotel boats," Symonette recalls, "main and jib, lots of bailing, but they taught us the basics. Patsy always led by example. She never asked you to do something she wouldn't do. She was a tomboy, mixed easily with the guys, and was physically very strong. A good seaman with tremendous balance. All of us looked up to her.

"She was racing cars back then, a real go-getter, the hit of the town. She'd drive by and we'd react—there goes Patsy Kenedy! She was not only good-looking but outward-going, and from an adventurous family. I had to admire her from afar. I was eight years younger, and that was a lot when you were a kid."

Patsy (left) with Paradise Island water-ski teammate
Gigi Macke, Miss Austria of 1964.

IV

BUSY

On Monday, February 11, 1963, the *Nassau Guardian* newspaper ran this grim lead headline on its front page: "Murder Probe After Man Is Found Dead." The man in question was Pat Kenedy's brother—Patsy's uncle—Campbell Greenidge. "The 56-year-old manager of Blackbeard's Tavern was found dead—believed to have been murdered," the story reported. "Police had to force their way into his home, and it is understood they found his body badly beaten." Both Greenidge's dalmatian dogs were also killed.

Robbery was suspected. It took two detectives from Scotland Yard weeks to apprehend two young Bahamian men. A trial was set. It was a nasty business that dominated the island's attention and provided still another emotional test of Pat Kenedy's fragile sensibility. She would have to testify at the trial, a duty she dreaded. "I can't understand why he should have been killed," Mrs. Kenedy was quoted in the *Guardian*. "Everyone liked him."

Always looking for a way to avoid Nassau's hot, dull summers, Patsy had planned a trip to Europe with a fellow water-skier, a woman named Lena. With Patsy's Yacht Haven apartment rent being covered by her parents, she'd been able to put money aside. She convinced her father to buy her Porsche. Then she ordered a new Volkswagen Variant to be picked up in the UK. The plan was to have the VW shipped back to Nassau after her trip and given to Lou in exchange for the Porsche—in time for Speed Week.

It all worked according to plan—except for Lena's boyfriend showing up at Heathrow when they landed. Surprise! He spirited Lena away (they would eventually marry), leaving Patsy without a fellow traveler to share expenses. "I bumped along," Patsy recalls. "There were good youth hostels back then. A dollar a night for a cot, a shower, and one meal. But they wouldn't take you if you had a car. I had to park way up the street."

It's apparent that Patsy Kenedy Bolling never spent more than a few minutes with anyone whose name and contacts she didn't record in a logbook. She started with scrapbooks as a child, and just kept at it. Amazingly, given Patsy's constant mobility, including many years living aboard a variety of boats, those logbooks were never lost or damaged along the way. Asked about a date, a name, or a situation, Patsy will often say she can look it up in the book. And she usually does. The fact that she drove to Austria to be in touch with Gigi (Gloria) Mackh, the 1964 Miss Austria who had been head of the water-ski shows at Paradise Island, is a good example. "Gigi and her family were wonderful," Patsy says. "They had a hotel on a lake. They took me in. I had to sleep in the attic, and they put me to work tending bar." The two women frequently went water-skiing. That led to meeting someone named Ralph, who was setting up the 1964 Olympics in Innsbruck for IBM. Ralph sent Patsy to see his mother, in Salzburg. "She had no English, I had no German," Patsy says, "but we got along famously. We drank slivovitz and threw the glasses into the fireplace." Patsy simply takes on whomever she is with.

******

In August, with the trial in Nassau revealing disturbing, intimate details of her brother's murder, Lou thought it best to get Pat out of town.

"Mommy lost the plot several times," Rosie says.

"Mommy didn't quite have a nervous breakdown," Patsy says. "But Daddy said she was sharp, uncontrollable, uncomfortable. He sent her to me in Europe."

For Patsy, some apprehension was involved. Their mother-daughter relationship had never been smooth. "I was always asking why," Patsy says. "I was a free spirit. I had Daddy's attention, and I used it. He paid more attention to me than to her. But having her along turned out to be great. We never had anything close to a warm relationship until that trip. Suddenly she was my pal, my traveling companion. We'd joke about what cheap hotel we could find next. She finally insisted we get a room with a toilet. We had some laughs. Plus Dad had sent her with some money. I was getting lean."

Brian Kenedy celebrating his enlistment in the US Navy.

The two women popped in on Brian, who was stationed in Villefranche on the French Riviera, in the Navy. From there they made side trips around Italy. They were in a theater watching *Wait Until Dark* when President John F. Kennedy was murdered. A week or two later, in Nassau, Patsy reclaimed her Porsche.

Low on funds after the Europe tour, she missed Speed Week. But she did get to meet the Beatles, who had been temporarily sequestered in Nassau while they were getting prepped for their presentation to the USA. Like all chambers of commerce, the Bahamas Development Board had red carpets at the ready when celebrities came to town. Most of those carpets were rolled out by a collection of attractive local women. Ever since she had so winningly accepted that Hard Lucky trophy after her Jaguar had caught fire during Speed Week, Miss Kenedy had been among the more recognizable young women in Nassau. She was called when it was time for the Beatles dinner.

She was scolded by the den mother when she showed up for the dinner on her father's Lambretta scooter, with her not-that-high heels in a shoulder bag. After running a comb through her hair and applying a bit of lipstick, she was admitted.

"They were nineteen," Patsy says of the Beatles. "Rude and crude. I thought they would be coy, just getting started. But they were already big in Europe. They were rough-cut. Smart alecks. They were all so cocky." Two weeks after that dinner, the Beatles' introduction to the USA on the Ed Sullivan Show on February 9, 1964, would go down as one of the most portentous music-group launches of all time.

The rest of that winter, Patsy taught sailing at Nassau's Montagu Beach Hotel, famous for its mermaid show patrons could watch though an underwater window in the lower bar, called the Jungle Club. The Montagu has long since been torn down. A fish market occupies the property.

Among Patsy's sailing students was a woman named Olive Adshead, a stewardess for Bahamas Airways. Olive had been working for Pan Am in London. She had used her discount airfares to visit Nassau. She loved it, and decided to stay. She and Patsy met at a party. Learning to sail followed.

"I had a vague idea about sailing," Olive says today from her home in the Azores, "but Patsy taught me the intricacies. One week there had been a dolphin swimming in the harbor. It made the news. They even named it. During one sailing lesson, there it was, near the boat. Patsy urged me to go to the bow for a closer look. I didn't realize what she had in mind. She rocked the boat, and suddenly I was swimming with the dolphin. I was petrified, shocked, but in the end the wonderful dolphin was swimming around and up against me, a good memory.

"We clicked," Olive says. "We were just two nice-look-ing young women having a good time. Those were fun days. We were fancy-free and doing everything we could

Olive Adshead (left) and Patsy having a reunion aboard Puritan *in 2017. They remain close friends.*

within the law." Olive says she became part of the Kenedy family, even working for Lou a few times when he needed a cook for his freighting trips to Miami. "He was a rough customer. But he was down to earth," Olive says. "So tightfisted. He'd steam stamps off envelopes if they hadn't been canceled. But you could tease him. He had a heart of gold. When he retired, he and Pat had a little cruise ship. Patsy and I liked to sunbathe without clothes on. Pat said, No, Daddy wouldn't like it. We had to comply.

"Patsy had plenty of boyfriends," Olive recalls, "but she was complaining she wasn't getting anywhere with them. The fact she could do most things better than men helped get her accepted as a competitor, but it was also a problem. I'm several years older, so I talked to her like a Dutch aunt. Patsy can do everything better than anyone else, be it mechanics, sailing, driving, or racing. I told her you've got to let your boyfriends be men.

"Once she had this new boyfriend. Six of us were in his outboard dinghy going to the beach. Her date was in charge, but he couldn't start the outboard. He pulled it and pulled it. I was sitting opposite Patsy and I was glaring at her because I knew her fingers were itching. I wanted her to be a lady for a change and let him figure it out. She couldn't contain herself. She jumped up, pulled the gas line out of the tank, sucked on it, put it back, pulled the rope, and off we went.

"With Bill Bolling," Olive says, "she finally met a man who could do as well as or a little better than her in many things. With Bill, Patsy finally met her match."

That would be several years down the road. Using Christmas as an emotional hook, Betty Bolling—Bill's first wife—had persuaded her rambling husband to have a visit from her and the children. Bill, who was still happily carrying on like a bachelor on his boat at Bahia Mar, rented a house for Christmas. It was a visit that would last six years.

At the time, Patsy's busy social life was focused on a sailor she'd met at one of the beach parties she'd initiated when the Southern Ocean Racing Conference (SORC), known as the Southern Circuit, came to town. In the 1960s, entries in the Circuit numbered close to a hundred, because there wasn't a better way on earth to race big boats and, for northerners especially, to escape the cold and have knock-down, drag-out, no-holds-barred parties with friends and competitors after racing all day under the hot sun.

The SORC was cleverly organized to allow owners and crews a chance to fly home and tend to business after the first two races, then return for the rest of the series. It was, as one participant put it, as much fun as you could have sailing. *Sports Illustrated*'s Coles Phinizy wrote about it in 1981: "There was a time long ago when the object of the SORC was simple: It was an excuse for salty chums to gather and try to win trophies and drink each other under the table."

The SORC was started in 1941, but the "time long ago" Phinizy was referring to was the 1960s, distance racing's golden age, before life got so data- and social-media-driven, when name designers like Charley Morgan (*Paper Tiger* for Jack Powell); Bill Tripp (*Ondine* for Huey Long); Sparkman & Stephens (many); Ted Hood (*Robin*, for himself); and builder Bob Derecktor (*Grey Goose*, for himself)—to mention a few—had boats primed for the first race from St. Petersburg to Miami. The boats would return to Saint Pete for the race to Fort Lauderdale that would follow.

After the break, the fleet of eighty to one hundred boats would race Miami to Nassau (a race down to only seventeen boats in 2024). The opportunity this presented to Patsy Kenedy was staggering. "Are you kidding me?" she says. "I got into car racing in December because there were three hundred good-looking men descending on Nassau. Now the SORC was coming in January with four hundred more good-looking men!"

Her objective was for more than dates. She wanted a berth on a race boat, not an easy goal. For women to be accepted racing cars was simple compared to women being allowed to crew on race boats in the thirty-five-to-seventy-foot range. Lack of strength was always the first reason given for keeping women off the boats. But everyone suspected that having a woman sharing a yacht's close quarters with a bunch of men for a distance race could be . . . disruptive.

Patsy had gone about getting berths in the usual way at the time: hanging out on the docks and being available. One talked the talk hoping for a chance to sail the sail and start building a portfolio of races on fast boats with positive feedback from owners and fellow crews. *Alpha*, the Kenedy family ketch, was moored at a busy dock in Nassau, a prime location for finding, in addition to Ted Turner, well-known boats being cleaned up between races. A few berths away lay *Gulfstream*, a seventy-foot cruising yawl. Patsy helped talk the owner into doing a local race, and got rave reviews.

Using the same approach, she did deliveries on the legendary Herreshoff ketch *Ticonderoga* (seventy-two feet LOA), and the equally famous yawl *Bolero* (seventy-two feet LOA). "I was always flaunting my body about, trying to get invited on a boat," Patsy says. "Whatever it took. I scrubbed fenders, I cooked, sewed sails, got my foot in the door until someone asked, Why is Patsy in the galley—she should be on deck. And I said, Of course, the deck is where I'm going."

What better way to put yourself in the thick of things than to throw a party? A party for sailors in those days, as Coles Phinizy suggested, was destined to expand the boundaries of unreasonable behavior. Owners hosting traditional, post-race crew dinners knew that damages might cost more than the food and drink. Some owners went so far as to encourage their crews to take it beyond the limits. Having a food fight, even a bench-clearing brawl, or drunken, overly enthused crewmen parading atop a table bearing the leftovers of thirty dinners at a five-star restaurant, was not uncommon. Alcohol was that much in charge of the game.

Her first party was a spontaneous effort. "There was no plan," Patsy says. "I just put out the word, arrived with my rum punch, and made everybody on the beach drunk. It was a good way to get everyone together, to be around the boat people, get myself involved." The following years the planning became important. The very coveted, handwritten invitations stating time (afternoon) and place and urging attendees to BYOB were hand-delivered to the boats. With the help of her girlfriends, Patsy organized live music, food, and her killer rum punch, all of which had to be transported by dinghy to beaches at the east end of Paradise Island. The bridge from the mainland was in place, but no paved roads had yet been built to the beaches.

Crews on the smaller boats arrived on their boats. Others rented dinghies. It was a mad scene. There was

Above: Kialoa II. Opposite page, top: Ticonderoga. Bottom: Bolero.
Patsy sailed on all three legendary yachts.

a bonfire, dancing, water-skiing, and spinnaker flying. Some nudity was evident. The most memorable event was a lively competition to find out how far a Boston Whaler could be driven up the beach. With the engine unlocked so it could flip up, the Whaler would be driven onto the beach at full speed. The driver who got the boat closest to the bonfire won. After each run, a gang of deliriously inebriated campers would drag the Whaler back to the water for the next contestant. At their height, fifty to a hundred sailors and friends attended these parties.

Pam Wall, who went on to be a cruising consultant and an advocate for women in sailing after circumnavigating the globe with her husband, Andy, has vivid memories of Patsy's SORC parties. Pam had met Patsy when she and Andy were cruising in the early 1970s. "We were anchored in Man-O-War Cay," Pam says. A big motor yacht called "*Pez Espada* came in, anchored upwind. I was making pancakes the next morning on a one burner, kerosene stove. Difficult stove to maneuver. I was burning the pancakes. I guess smoke must have been coming out of the hatch. Suddenly I heard this outboard racing toward us, bumping alongside, and there's Patsy jumping aboard with a fire extinguisher. She's thinking the boat is on fire. I was so embarrassed. But that's Patsy in a nutshell. Ready to help people. Always there with the right things. Very intelligent woman. And in those days, there weren't many."

But the nature of Patsy's SORC parties shocked Pam. "I was an innocent young girl," Pam says today. "My parents were teetotalers. I didn't drink. My idea of a party was at the Chicago Yacht Club with blazers and dresses.

I can't explain how wild the beach parties were. I hadn't met Patsy then. But I was watching people who I knew and liked quite well act like I couldn't believe. It was like looking at a bad movie. I'd never been exposed to anything like it. It was more excessive than I wanted to see."

Paige Neuberth helped Patsy put the parties togeth-

er. After college, Paige had taught English as a second language in elementary school before taking a job at Lilly Pulitzer's women's shop in Palm Beach. She says a boat-related weekend in Jamaica permanently changed her life for the better. She had met Patsy along the way, and they had clicked. "I don't know why," Paige says, "preppy girl that I was, meeting Patsy with her F-bomb. In those days people just didn't use that word, and of course it's the second word that comes out of her mouth. That F-bomb. My God. It's so funny. She was just fresh, not nasty. Funny! And she had no qualms about taking her top off. That used to get some attention.

"She didn't suffer fools, men or women. She was never

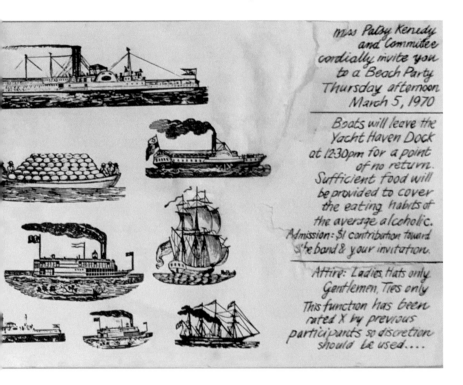

miss Patsy Kenedy and Committee cordially invite you to a Beach Party Thursday afternoon March 5, 1970

Boats will leave the Yacht Haven Dock at 12:30pm for a point of no return. Sufficient food will be provided to cover the eating habits of the average alcoholic. Admission: $1 contribution toward the band & your invitation.

Attire: Ladies, Hats only. Gentlemen, Ties only. This function has been rated X by previous participants so discretion should be used....

rude or mean. If you weren't secure in your own position, she didn't hurt you. She just dismissed you. It's the way she was. She taught me a lot. I hadn't grown up sailing. She was so rugged in shorts and a T-shirt. So tough. Later we did some deliveries together. She taught me to be prepared for anything. She had these hiding places on the boat. When it was time to hit the yacht club for awards ceremonies, out would come a pair of high heels from a nook under the dining table. Out of another corner would come a sexy little dress. Patsy who was so rough-and-tumble would hit the runway, I'm telling you, with a big splash. When the cameras came out she'd be front and center. She taught me how to hide my dressy clothes.

"There was so much alcohol at those SORC parties," Paige says. "But there were no games, no tug-of-wars, no competitions other than the Whaler thing. And no drugs, not back then. Lucky. Or cell phones. No pictures! That was lucky too. Just people standing around on the beach talking and getting very drunk. Driving the Whaler onto the beach was memorable. Lucky no one got hurt. But it was mainly a drinking afternoon out in the sun."

Getting the boats back to Nassau Harbour after the party was always a challenge, especially the time when a couple jokers had dived on several of the boats and tied their folding propellers closed.

The parties worked for Patsy. They had her name all over them, establishing her as both an enthusiastic host-ess and a force to be reckoned with. Her parties would go on with increasing attendance and more hell-bent energy after every Miami-to-Nassau race until 1970.

At one party, Patsy met a sailor she liked well enough to follow to California. It was summer, after all. Nothing much going on in Nassau. She shipped her Porsche to Florida on her father's boat and hit the road. One would assume her relationship with the sailor had to be on the serious side to create such an effort on her part. But she says no. It was simply adventure, and the sailor's promise of good sailing to be had on larger boats. "I never thought any relationship was going to be *it*," Patsy says. "I wasn't into marriage. It was never in my thoughts. In the '60s, many women were looking to get married. Not me. Didn't want any part of it. If you don't want kids, and I never did, there's no reason to get married."

California didn't work out. The relationship quickly fizzled. Worse than that, the sailing didn't materialize. Patsy ended up working at a Denny's and renting a house with a coworker. "My sailor friend did introduce me to Freddie Schenck," she says, "an older guy who had won two Snipe nationals as crew (1954 and '55), and one as skipper ('57)." Schenck had a yacht-brokerage business out of which he was selling Victory sloops, twenty-one-foot daysailers. He hired Patsy to teach people how to sail them, and often put her on board boats cruising to Catalina Island.

"It wasn't what I'd call exciting," Patsy says. "I wasn't happy. I wanted to go sailing, go wherever the guys were going, and it wasn't working in California. I was a waitress at a breakfast joint, and babysitting people's kids on boats. I had so much going for me in Nassau. I was a queen back there. I could do anything I wanted, when I wanted, with who I wanted. And I had family to back me up, bounce things off. I could get back into the car racing."

By the time she had organized her departure, driven back cross-country, and flown over to Nassau, she'd missed Speed Week 1963. But she got her first look at Bill Bolling. Her father had picked up another boat, one of sixty fast eighty-three-foot motor vessels that had been originally designed and built to support the Normandy invasion. Lou had bought number four, called *Aquanaut*, and had chartered it to Ivan Tors, the producer of the *Flipper* series. Tors was shooting *Thunderball* at the time.

Patsy as a stewardess for Bahamas Air in 1965.

Bill was working as a support diver. Patsy, Rosie, and Ga-brielle jumped on board *Aquanaut* whenever they could to watch the filming, ogle the stars, and be ready if they were asked to be extras. "I saw Bill," Patsy says, "but I was dating another diver at the time."

When Lou chartered *Aquanaut* to Columbia University to install some Decca navigation systems in the islands, there was fun to be had with the young scientists working the job. "I didn't date them," Patsy says, "but they were great guys who often took me for dinners and dancing." The head of the project came at Patsy with a more serious proposition. Realizing her potential, he offered her a full scholarship at Columbia to study the science behind what they were doing. "I saw Daddy's eyes light up," Patsy says today. "We talked. I reminded him I don't see well, I don't read ahead like other people, for me it's one word at a time. It would be mostly memorizing, and they'd be paying my way. I'd be marrying them, making a commitment, living in New York and commuting for four years. What happens if I don't like it after a year? I couldn't quit. I'd have to stick with it because that's what I do. I had finished school. Finished it. Done." Lou understood.

She might have missed Speed Week, but she was in time to host another SORC party, always a good time. And thanks to her friendship with Olive Adshead, she landed a job as a stewardess (what flight attendants were called in 1965) at Bahamas Air. The fact that Bahamas Air had to drastically reduce their number of flights and staff in the summer months turned out to be perfect for Patsy's adventure schedule.

Being an airline employee enabled her to buy plane tickets at a discount, a situation that came in handy when her friend, an enthusiastic racer chaser by the name of (the late) B. J. Beach, suggested they should hop on Pan Am 001, a flight around the world. Leaving from San Francisco, Pan Am 001 stopped in Honolulu, Hong Kong,

Bangkok, Delhi, Beirut, Istanbul, Frankfurt, London, and New York. All for $2,300 per person (ten times that in 2024 dollars). Side trips were permitted as long as one completed the schedule in 180 days. With Patsy's discount, tickets were $1,800.

With side trips included, the trip took six months. By definition, adventures don't often go as planned. Patsy started off with a boyfriend she ditched in Greece. "I couldn't stand the guy one more minute," she says today. "He gave me my ticket and five hundred dollars and went away." Patsy's notes from the trip are reminiscent of her father's initial voyage on his first schooner: African buses bearing people's goats and hens stopping every hour to allow passengers to pee on the road; checking shoes for scorpions; being habitually broke; and frequently sleeping on a cot in B. J's and her partner's hotel room. On the bright side, there was also a cruise down the Nile, and the essential riding of camels. All in all, the trip was considered a great success. Best of all, Patsy made it home in time for Speed Week (heat 1 of Locals, second of ten cars; heat 2 of Locals, third of nine cars). And Gabrielle's wedding.

Patsy touching up the paint on 12-Meter **American Eagle** *before the Trans-Atlantic race in 1969.*

V

CREWING

In the mid-'60s, Patsy began making her way as a sailor. She had managed to get on board *Kialoa*, one of the more formidable maxi yachts, for a delivery. "Owner Jim Kilroy always made it a point to say hello to me and ask when I would be on board again." And once again her popular SORC party had produced a romance, this time with a highly regarded sailor named John Rumsey. The son of an engineer who migrated West in the '30s to help build the Bay Bridge, Rumsey was born in San Francisco. "Socially," says Rumsey, who turned eighty-seven in 2023, "in those days you could join either the volunteer fire company or the yacht club. Dad chose the San Francisco Yacht Club, so I learned to sail."

John Rumsey, a love interest of Patsy's in the late 1960s.

Rumsey raced 5.5-meters, then an Olympic class (he would win the world championship as crew in 1980), and Star boats. He built a Star because all his friends had one. The Star is an old, well-organized one-design class. It's a demanding, two-man boat that has managed to stay current without losing its unique lines or classic character. Founded in 1911, this class has always attracted the best sailors in the world. Racing a Star put Rumsey in touch with the class's habitual master, the late Lowell North, who incredibly won five Star World Championships between 1945 and 1973. More amazing, North placed second in the Worlds seven times. He also won an Olympic gold medal in the Star in 1968.

When North started his well-known sail-making company in the late 1950s, he hired Rumsey as his production manager. The two men had gotten to be friends racing Stars, and as Rumsey says with a laugh, "I had beaten him in a few sailboat races." Rumsey became one of North's "Tigers," the name given to the hot, aggressive sailors North hired to promote and sell his brand by helping race their customers' boats to podium positions. "I traveled all over the country, all over the world," Rumsey says. "I worked in lofts in Oregon, Munich . . . I got to sail with the best sailors in the world. It was a continuous adventure."

When Patsy met Rumsey, he was sales manager of North's main loft in San Diego. That meant another trip to California. This time, the relationship was the priority, but Rumsey's connections suited her just fine. She arrived in San Diego in July 1967 to find that Rumsey was off on the Transpac race from Los Angeles to Honolulu. She flew to Honolulu to find a happy crew. In a light air race that favored the smaller boats, their Cal 40, named *Holiday Too*, had won Class C and corrected first in fleet. Patsy and Rumsey cruised the islands, then flew back to San Diego.

"There was a party at Lowell's," Rumsey recalls. Cy Gillette, a prominent Star sailor who would go on to be a yachting judge, was there. "Patsy went to find the bathroom," Rumsey says. "Cy's wife Camille was just leaving. She asked Patsy if Lou Kenedy, with one 'N,' was her father. Patsy said yes. It turned out that back a few years Camille was in the islands somewhere, met Lou, and they were an item. All that in Lowell's bathroom.

"We drove cross-country in the Porsche," Rumsey says. "Patsy and me and a Siamese cat, which was kind of a pain." They stopped in Newport, Rhode Island, to spend time with pals of Rumsey who were crewing on the 12-meters *Intrepid*, *Columbia*, and *American Eagle*, sailors who were busy competing to defend the America's Cup. In those days, helmets weren't required, and crews had active social lives. *Intrepid* (skipper Bus Mosbacher) would get the job done that year, winning the right to defend the Cup and defeating Australia's *Dame Pattie* (skipper Jock Sturrock) in the best-of-seven match. Hanging out with a bunch of America's Cup sailors was excellent for Patsy's logbook.

Pike's Arm, *the old freighter owned by Lou Kenedy.*

Back in Florida, Patsy and Rumsey did a few trips on *Pike's Arm*, a cranky old eighty-foot freighter Lou Kenedy had picked up to lug essential goods (including rum, of course) between Miami and the out islands—Spanish Wells and Harbour Island. That November, Rumsey headed for Freeport, Grand Bahama, an island 130 miles northwest of Nassau, to take part in one of the great maxi-boat stories unfolding on a Freeport beach.

The 1960s, '70s, and '80s were the golden days of distance racing, a time when a who's who niche of mostly male captains of industry took their grand sporting ambitions to sea. They poured big money and applied their clever minds into having fast yachts designed and built. They sought out the most talented sailors to sail them, and led the charge into blue water. The competition was as intense on the ocean as it was in their boardrooms. Ocean racing became a seductive subculture, attracting sailors from all over the world who were eager to attach themselves to the otherwise unreachable boats of their fantasies.

Like sharks and pilot fish, owners and crews on race boats are strange bedfellows. The toleration factor has to be extended on both sides. The more capable sailors have to accommodate their owners' whims while not so subtly but also politely asserting themselves and taking charge of racing the yachts. The owners have to be willing to leave their titles and corporate egos on the docks, and agree to yield to the expertise of those often rough-and-tumble swabbies. It is symbiosis to the max. When crews vary between eight on the smaller boats to twenty-plus on the maxis, the complex dynamics resulting are tenuously held together by the common goal of surviving what the sea dishes out, and, that done, of winning. It doesn't always work. When it does, strong, loyal teams laced with pride are the result.

In those golden days, other than the full-time captains and mates who ran the boats, most of the swabbies didn't get paid. The late Jim Kilroy, who got high marks as owner of *Kialoa*, required his crews to buy their own plane tickets as a statement of their commitment. Once aboard, he covered their expenses.

Perhaps no owner got into the ocean-racing game as stylishly as the late Robert Johnson, a lumber magnate who happened to own properties—a Chart House restaurant and some housing—in Freeport, Grand Bahama. Johnson had been bitten by the ocean-racing bug, having sailed on the esteemed *Stormvogel*, Cornelius Bruynzeel's original maxi (LOA 74.6", 1959), and the legendary *Ticonderoga*. In 2024, both are still competing. Having chartered *Ticonderoga*, Johnson was so enthralled by the boat he bought the Herreshoff–designed ketch by phone, halfway to Hawaii during the 1963 Transpac race. Randall Peffer's elegant book, *Windward Passage,* relates how Johnson hired the young Alan Gurney to design a yacht of that name the size of *Ticonderoga*, only faster: lighter, with a modern underbody.

Shunning aluminum, Johnson decided to build the boat out of top-grade Sitka spruce and Douglas fir, of which he had lots. He hired a couple builders he admired from California, and recruited a workforce of a dozen sailors from *Ticonderoga*'s crew. The builders poured a concrete plate on the beach and got to work. Some of the crew worked at the Chart House nights. Most of them lived in the apartments Johnson owned.

Patsy was a frequent weekend visitor to the project, deadheading over from Nassau on Bahamas Air to see John Rumsey. But their relationship cooled off. "I'm not sure why," she says. "I think it was geographically inconvenient. He was probably dating in Freeport. It didn't end angrily. It just petered out. We are good friends to this day." That was an unfortunate development, because Patsy and the crew had become mates. She would have been a natural addition to *Windward Passage*, a boat that came off the beach like a shot, fast and competitive from the outset. But it turned out that John Rumsey would become *Windward Passage*'s captain. Having his ex-girlfriend on the crew wouldn't have worked.

But Patsy had polished the rap every sailor in search of a berth cultivates to break the ice coating the first step for getting on a race boat. It has to be a carefully construct-ed line of conversation aimed at drawing out the guy next

Patsy (red hat) worked the crowd at a party on Kialoa II when notable yachts (Eagle at left) rafted after the 1969 Jamaica Race.

to you in a sailor's bar who's been identified as important, while subtly letting him know you have also sailed some serious miles. "Subtly" is the key word. Bragging doesn't do it. Sounding quietly confident is good. Humor works.

You're in a bar, after all. If you happened to be a woman in those days, a woman casting about for a berth in a men's sport, it helped to be on the attractive side, and with a few muscles showing.

It worked, getting Patsy aboard *Kialoa* for several deliveries and eventually for the race from St. Petersburg to Venice, Florida. As cook. And as the one who drove the boat's rental car to ferry crew to the airport. "I didn't mind," Patsy says today. "It was a foot in the door."

That led to a berth on *Yankee Girl*, a forty-eight-footer owned by Dallas oilman David Steere, for the Miami-to-Nassau race. The problem was that *Yankee Girl* wasn't doing the following race to Jamaica. More walking and talking was necessary. *Solution*, a tasty fifty-footer, happened to be at the Harbour Club dock in Nassau, across the street from Patsy's apartment. She cruised by, recognized a couple crewmen she'd met at a party. They invited her on board. They chatted. The owner, Thor Ramsing, an investor with ties to the Huntington Hartford family (A&P supermarkets and Paradise Island), came on deck. "One guy says, Jesus, Thor, we need a good-looking cook on this boat. Why don't we get Patsy to come on the Jamaica Race? The other says, And she can sail. Thor says, Sure, are you up for that? And I said, Yes, as long as you pay my way home. He says, Hmm, I don't know. Then he says, We're coming right back, you can come with us. I said, Okay, let's do that."

The race went well, but *Solution* would be sailing back without Patsy. There was too much fun to be had in Jamaica. "One day someone rented a bus," Patsy recalls, "and we all piled on. There was Ted Turner, and Bob Johnson from

Passage, and Huey Long from *Ondine*, a bunch of sailors, and way too much booze. We went to various beaches, fell in the water, got back on the bus, had another drink, listened to Turner carrying on. At one point I remember Turner and Johnson seeing who could piss highest up a wall. Needless to say we were all quite drunk."

With *Solution* about to depart, Patsy needed a bunk, and a ride back to Miami. That was when Paige Neuberth met her. "A friend of my dad's was doing the race to Jamaica," Paige says. "We decided to fly down and meet them. Turns out her dad had abandoned the race. Suddenly we had no place to stay. We didn't know anyone. We went to the yacht club and met a great gang of people. We ended up in sleeping bags on *American Eagle*'s deck. Ted Turner's boat. His guy Jimmy Brown cooked us breakfast. Then this woman appeared, coming up the swim ladder. She'd just swum over from *Solution* to see what was going on. It was Patsy."

Patsy had long set her sights on the sixty-seven-foot, Bill Luders–designed 12-meter that had failed to win the right to defend the America's Cup in both 1964 and 1967 while attracting a lot of fans. She doesn't really know why, other than that she liked the boat's lines, and perhaps because it was owned by Turner, whom she had "dated" once. She'd kept up with Turner's exploits when he had been in Nassau racing 5.5s, but had not seen him socially. She'd also kept up with *Eagle*, which had been winning more than its share of races since Turner had bought it in 1968. Turner was serious about winning the World Ocean Racing Championship, meaning the boat had a heavy schedule, including a transatlantic race. "And the captain was a good-looking guy," Patsy adds.

"Patsy was fun," Paige Neuberth says, "nice. We hit it off. I flew back. She ended up sailing back to Lauderdale on *Eagle*."

"I got a bunk on *Eagle*," Patsy says today. "There were just two crew left on the boat. The captain, the late David Andre, was one. I was just sleeping on the boat. I was gone all day, spinnaker flying on *Kialoa*, going to Ocho Rios, having a good time. David needed crew to take *Eagle* back to the States. It was eight hundred miles, would take five days or a week. I was broke. Didn't have a nickel. I said I'd help. He got one more person, and the four of us took *Eagle* to Lauderdale."

A racing crew on a 12-meter numbers twelve. Even in scaled-down cruising trim, a 12-meter is a lot of boat for four people to handle. Patsy showed David Andre that she could do it.

A week or so after they arrived, Patsy was cruising down the Miami River on *Pike's Arm*, earning a little money working for her father. Patsy was at the helm because Lou was temporarily disabled. He'd had major back surgery: the removal of five vertebrae. A prolonged recovery had kept him in the hospital for three months. Lou was strapped into a bunk in the pilothouse behind Patsy, unable to move but still the captain. It wasn't fun. "I was nervous," Patsy says. "Driving a piece of shit like *Pike's Arm* on the Miami River was tough. *Pike's* top speed was eight knots. It wouldn't back or maneuver. Holding your position while waiting for bridges to open was damn near impossible. The river was narrow, with current. Cuban boats tied to trees hindered visibility."

Opposite page: **Patsy says she was comfortable aboard the maxi, Kialoa II.** *Owner Jim Kilroy made her feel welcome.*

Patsy was in a bikini, her usual working uniform. The Dupont Plaza Hotel and marina were coming up to port, and there, moored to the dock, were several of the larger race boats, including the familiar profile of *American Eagle*. Suddenly the day seemed a little brighter. With

Patsy with old friends Paige Neuberth (above), and Ted Turner at his 75th birthday party.

Captain Lou grumbling about her slowing down, Patsy brought *Pike's Arm* to a crawl, then stopped it, more or less, within hollering distance of *Eagle*. She hailed Turner, who was on deck.

"I said, Ted, hey Ted, I want to go on *Eagle* for a race. And he says, No, no women on this boat. No women! The other guys on *Eagle* are looking cross-eyed at him, not believing what he just said, here's this gal in a bikini, and you're not going to take her on board?"

Later that week Patsy again approached Turner, at a party at Coral Gables Yacht Club, about getting on the boat, and he was adamant. "He said, No, final answer, I'm not taking you."

The next day Patsy was back on *Pike's Arm*, making a beeline for Dupont Plaza. This time David Andre was the only one on board. "I knew he had to take the boat north," Patsy says. "I also knew he liked what I could do on the boat. I asked him when he was leaving. He said in four days. He said it was okay if I wanted to come. He'd test me some more on the way to Savannah and if it worked out I could stay on for a while. And I'm saying to myself, My foot is in the door! He asked me how much I was making on *Pike's*. I said fifty dollars a week. He said, Okay, fifty dollars a week."

When Patsy showed up on *Eagle* four days later with seabag in hand, surprise—Ted Turner was on board. He'd be sailing to Savannah. "Ted was okay," Patsy said. "I'm sure David had sung my praises to him. We took off. I steered some, was in charge of the backstays. My presence was never discussed again. I became part of the wood-work. It was two or three days to Savannah, a nothing trip. I showed them what I could do, be on top of things and get stuff done before anyone had to tell me. Eye for the job. It's not how strong you are on a boat that counts. It's the timing. Get the timing right and not so much muscle is needed. Jimmy Brown, Ted's all-purpose valet since childhood, was cooking. Jimmy was a beautiful man. He told me it was good to have a woman on board because it didn't smell so bad down below."

"David told me Ted ended up trusting Patsy, appreciated her talent," Paige says. "He told me Ted said if you're doing a delivery and all hell breaks loose in the middle of the night, Patsy could go up and handle any position on the boat."

"In Savannah I stayed on," Patsy says, "making my way each day, finding jobs to do. I sewed some sails, painted the boot top, painted the cockpit. Finally, David said I was on for the New York delivery, fifty dollars a week. I said I didn't want to be on as cook. David said no, I didn't have to cook. Jimmy Brown was coming with us. Thank you, Jesus."

How well Patsy integrated herself on *Eagle* can be measured by the trick Turner and the crew played on her as they approached Mamaroneck, New York, the site of the late Bob Derecktor's northern boatyard. In a world of rough customers on the hard side of yachting, Bob Derecktor stood out. Legend had it Derecktor ate nails for lunch and tossed at least one company president a week out of his yard for having the gall to inquire about the progress of his million-dollar boat Bob was building. Bob's print ad in *Yachting Magazine* read, "When accepting phone calls conflicts with building boats, Bob Derecktor tends to build boats."

Derecktor had built his first boat as a teenager. He dug a hole in his family's yard and got his father to help him pour a lead keel. A tireless worker from the old school with a keen mind and skilled hands, Bob began his day by rowing four miles to work in a fast pulling boat

Irascible boat builder, Bob Derecktor.

he'd designed and built. Under six feet tall and powerfully built, Bob had wrestled at Yale before dropping out. He dressed the part, with a wool cap pulled over his large head and red-white-and-blue suspenders stretched over his barrel chest. He usually had a chip balanced on one shoulder. Patience was a foreign object for Bob as he stormed around his yard every day running a one-man show involving the direction of several boats under construction, designing and fabricating hardware, managing purchasing, and taking twelve minutes for lunch.

Turner, who'd enjoyed many an amusing, pitched go-round with Derecktor, thought it would be fun to send the unwitting Patsy in to see Bob when they arrived, bearing a bunch of caustic messages that were guaranteed to piss him off. "Ted prepped me to meet him," she says. "I got dressed for the role, wearing my red hat and suspenders. Ted said to give Bob a rasher of shit, like how come there was no one to greet us and help us tie up when we arrived, what kind of sorry-ass operation are you running here, and where's our mail?—barge in and kick ass.

"I walked in and said to Rosie, his secretary, I wanted to see Bob. She said, Who are you, he's busy. I made a fuss. He comes out of his office and says, Who are you? I say, Who are you, because I had no idea. And he says, I'm Bob Derecktor. And I said, Oh, I'm Patsy Kenedy and I've been sent here to ask why no one was out there to take our lines, and I ranted on, snapping my suspenders. He's leaning up against the doorjamb cheekily smiling and shuffling papers in his hands and I'm going on about what a lax scene it is, and he says, Well, fine, how do you do, and we're not a marina, you know, we're boatbuilders, and he went into a huff. I put out my hand and said, Ted put me up to this. You're a good guy and let's get on with it."

They became tight friends, Patsy and Bob. *Eagle* was in the yard for a month. When *Eagle* wasn't racing locally, on weekends, David Andre and Patsy would race on *Salty Goose* (fifty-six feet LOA), the fourth boat Derecktor had built for himself, one that would win her class in the 1975 SORC. Patsy soon realized Derecktor was cut from the same rugged cloth as her father. "Bob was so gruff, so tough. He'd kick guys in the ass. Why are two guys carrying this plank? Gimme that, I can do it myself. He was uncompromising. Both Lou and Bob did whatever they needed to do to get it done. They didn't give a shit about the law." The difference was that Bob Derecktor didn't shoot anyone, not that we know.

Jim Mattingly worked for Derecktor for fourteen years. He has a good laugh when he recalls Patsy showing up dressed like his boss. "Patsy got along with Bob, with men in general," Mattingly says, "because she wasn't afraid to do anything. She did whatever was asked of her. And she was a good listener. That made her a welcome part of any team. And it made her a great learner. You didn't have to explain things to Patsy twice. She'd figure it out. And she never contradicted anyone. She just took it all in, evaluated it, and made a decision."

Patsy remembers being in the yard one Sunday and hearing hammer blows echoing in the quiet of the big shed. She followed the sound and found Bob having a parental visit with his two daughters, ages six and eight. He was teaching them to drive and extract nails. "He was only slightly embarrassed," Patsy says. "He just shrugged and said, It's a good thing for them to learn to do, isn't it?"

******

Patsy was confirmed as a crew on *Eagle* for the 1969 transatlantic race from Newport to Cork, Ireland. Her assignment was handling the running backstays and

other jobs in the back of the boat, leaving the big "coffee grinder" winches to the strong guys. Although when it was necessary, she could turn those handles. Giving her the backstays was testament to the degree of confidence Turner and Andre had in Patsy's ability. *Eagle* had a permanent backstay hitched to the masthead. The "runners" attached to the mast three-quarters of the way up. They

Opposite page: American Eagle *charges upwind.* **Above:** *Patsy on* **Eagle's** *afterdeck during the La Rochelle Race in 1969.*

were secured to the deck near the rail on each side of the boat, aft of the wheel, with a multipart wire rig that led through a block on the deck to a large winch. The runners were essential for altering sail shape via mast bend and for mast stability. "They were a very important item for this boat," Patsy says today. "That mast looked like a wet noodle at times."

During tacks and jibes, easing the old runner as the boom passed amidships and securing the new runner before the new tack was fully established required perfect timing and fast hands. Several hard turns with a winch handle—in low gear—would fine-tune the tension between ten thousand and twenty-thousand pounds. Fail to get the new runner up on time, and in the right sequence, and the mast could go over the side.

The transatlantic race was one of five required races to be completed over a three-year period for boats competing in the initial World Ocean Racing Championship. Since Turner had bought the boat in 1969, *American Eagle* had been in the thick of it. The race turned out to be mostly uneventful, although halfway across the Atlantic the bolt that passed through the mast below the spreaders to hold the lower shrouds in place broke. The port upper shroud, a rod, went snaking down to the deck and bounced overboard. The spinnaker was up at the time, pulling the mast forward and putting pressure on both lower shrouds, which angle slightly aft. Fortunately, the wind speed was under twelve knots, and the sea state was reasonable.

"Ted was on deck ordering lines to be rigged to take the strain off the mast," Patsy says. The spinnaker was struck to ease the forward pressure. Both backstays were quickly tensioned. "A guy named Jim Brass was hauled up to make a diagnosis," Patsy says. "The hole in the mast was now egg-shaped, elongated from the bolt working against the mast. Trying to pass a bolt through the mast once the starboard shroud was connected was a bitch. To do the job Jim needed a one-inch bolt ten inches long, threaded at both ends. We scrambled through the boat to find something that would work. Lordy, we found two one-inch pieces. And we had a spare lower rod. Using the longer piece we were able to make the repair in two hours, with lots of rags and sealant used to cover the oversized hole in the mast. We got a jib up in the meantime, so we only lost a couple knots of boat speed."

The fact that Turner and his crew had decided to take a boat designed as a daysailer to race around buoys into the ocean was risky business. It's lucky, as Patsy says, A. E. Luders built *Eagle* "like a brick shithouse." A wooden boat, her frames were quite small, but they were on six-inch centers. There were scary moments. "We put the bow under to the mast several times," Patsy says. "The tension, the vibration, was an eerie feeling. The load at the mast step had to be incredible. The boat had never seen anything like that. I bunked in the forepeak and it often felt like the bow was going to break off. I told the guys if it does, grab my feet and pull me out."

But she says *Eagle* was a joy to handle, and praises Turner's prowess at the helm. "Ted would come on watch, take the wheel, and after a few minutes of tweaking this or that he'd have the boat going a knot or so faster. He concentrated. Upwind he had it dialed in. Downwind he'd get bored, lose concentration, start quoting Shakespeare or going on about famous sea battles."

One of Patsy's jobs on the boat was making sure everyone's gear was properly stowed. She let everyone know that items left lying about would go overboard, and she meant it. Two or three crewmen lost shoes or boots. The crew quietly began planning its revenge.

Eagle would win her class in the race, and take third overall, keeping her well in the hunt for the WORC crown. But to Turner's annoyance, it was Patsy the Irish press was interested in. Under the headline "Patsy joins the Sea Dogs," the story in the *Cork Examiner* read: "A lone pretty girl on a twelve-day passage with thirteen men . . . landed at the Royal Cork Yacht Club's brand new floating pontoon this weekend after rapid crossing of the Atlantic under sail . . . Any problems crossing the Atlantic with thirteen men? we asked her. 'No problems at all,' she said. 'I think a girl on an ocean racer is great for the morale of the crew.'"

"Patsy is a great crew," said *American Eagle*'s navigator, David Andre, of New Orleans. "She has sailed as many miles as most of the other crewmembers." A picture of Patsy at *Eagle*'s helm ran with the story.

No sooner had they finished than *Eagle* was off on the Skag Race, a triangle that included marks off Denmark, Norway, and Sweden. The very light wind condition was bugging Turner. He had a 5.5-meter regatta scheduled. The lack of wind was going to cause him to miss it. He was frantic. He demanded the rubber dinghy be inflated so he could row ashore. "Our navigator, Peter Bowker, appeared on deck with the rule book stating a vessel had to finish with the same number of crew it started with," Patsy says. "That was that. Ted missed the regatta. He was tearing his hair out."

Setting a new course record for the Fastnet Race—a seven-hundred-mile jaunt starting in Cowes, UK, rounding Fastnet Rock in the Irish Sea, and finishing (then) in Plymouth, UK—finishing first in class, and winning more than his share of races during Cowes Week would ease the pain.

Turner flew home. What was left of the crew took *Eagle* to Belém, Portugal, a historically glamorous neighborhood in Lisbon on the Tagus River, for an overhaul. The interior was stripped and repainted, causing the crew

First Fastnet race arrival in Plymouth was American Eagle, and on board today are Ma Cunningham, Patsy Kenedy, Peter Bowker and R E Turner III, who is the owner.

Lucky 13 As Patsy Joins The "Sea Dogs"

A LONE pretty girl on a 12 ...' passage with 13 men ... the proprietor of an exclusive .... restaurant in New York turned acht's cook ... and a company executive who is considering bringing his fellow board members from California to Cork for a meeting . . . these are some of the interesting people who landed at the Royal Cork Yacht Club's brand new floating pontoon this week-end after rapid crossings of the Atlantic under sail. Three big racing yachts have brought 46 crew members to Crosshaven as the transatlantic race from Newport, Rhode Island, nears its end. Each one has its story.

Patsy Kennedy (25) has relatives somewhere in this country and she may even find time to say a quick "Hello there" to some. Salt water runs in her veins because her father is a sailing ship skipper of yesteryear. She has sailed everything from dinghies up to three-masters. Now she has helped

bring a 12-metre yacht across 2,750 miles of Atlantic.

"Any problems in crossing the Atlantic with 13 men?—No problems at all. I think a girl on board an ocean racer is great for the morale of a crew."

"Patsy is a great crew," said American Eagle's navigator, David Andre of New Orleans. "She has sailed as many miles as most of the other crew members."

Mr. Andre also related that American Eagle's weather man, Dick Grossmuller, kept up serenades between watches below decks on a harmonica. Ondine, first yacht to finish, had cordon bleu cooking. Presiding in her galley was Charles Masson, proprietor of La Grenouille restaurant, one of the most exclusive and expensive in New York. Never did an Atlantic crew do so well. "He

gave us the most incredibly good menus," said his friend and skipper, Sumner A. "Huey" Long, a New York tanker broker. Both John "but I am called Jim" Kilroy and his friend and navigator, Patrick Reynolds, are of Irish extraction. The skipper's father was born in Dublin but basically his family are from Cork. Mr. Reynolds' father was from Westmeath and his mother from Waterford. He knows Ireland well because as navigation superintendent for Pan-American Airways he has spent a lot of time at Shannon Airport. He has also taken part in four Fastnet races.

Mr. Kilroy reckons his yacht has sailed 100,000 miles in five years with 50 per cent wins on corrected times. He is the head of a big property and investment company in Los Angeles and is considering whether he should return there for a board meeting or invite his directors to join him for their meeting in Ireland.

to bounce around looking for bunks. Patsy got situated on *Kialoa*, which was docked nearby. "We made a hit by showing the movies I'd shot on the way across.

"We had no money," Patsy recalls. "We waited for money from Ted forever. It seemed like we were always hanging around the American Express office waiting for money. Getting money out of him was like pulling teeth. He was just getting CNN going. He'd say, My kids are going barefoot so you all can sail my boat around. We pooled what we had to keep the boat going."

They sailed south to Las Palmas in the Canary Islands, their jumping-off port for the trip back across the Atlantic, waiting for October weather to set sail. And money. "Finally six hundred arrived," Patsy says. "Not enough for fuel after the bills were paid. We came across with no engine, no generator. I had a flashlight attached to my head to cook, used canned food out of the bilge with no labels. We had five or ten dozen eggs. Every two or three days we'd turn the eggs to keep the yolks from leaning against the membrane. I learned that from Lou."

They also fished. One day they hauled in a dozen dolphins, one of the tastiest fish in the sea, along with clumps of seaweed. A seaweed fight ensued. "A while later," Patsy says, "I'm in the head and I see this crab crawling on my crotch. Holy shit, I've got crabs! What do I do? Everything is open with these guys, we're all naked half the time, having showers. I go on deck and say, I think I have crabs. Oh my God, Patsy, they say, you better shave. So I do. They said, There's no medicine, better use vinegar. Okay. Now I'm burning from the vinegar. They're laughing. As the hair grows back it's itching. They say, You better shave again.

"When we got to Barbados they told me they made sure there was a crab in the clump of seaweed they shoved down my bikini bottom. It was payback. I didn't know how big crabs were, never had them. This one was big as my thumbnail. I had no idea the real ones were so small. There was no Google in those days to find out about stuff like that."

When they got back, Turner wanted to do the race from St. Petersburg to Isla Mujeres, across the Gulf of Mexico to an island off the tip of the Yucatan Peninsula. "I had to cook on that one," Patsy says. "Jimmy Brown was absent. Ted told me he'd pay me a little extra to cook. He kept ragging on that bit about his kids going barefoot. I told him my heart was bleeding."

Then there was the Lipton Cup, fourth of the six races that made up the 1970 SORC: a twenty-five-mile race around the buoys off Miami. Shortly after the start, *Eagle* and Huey Long's *Ondine* were close aboard, hard on the wind, just off the beach. It was blowing twenty. *Ondine* tacked away. Ahead, *Eagle*'s bowman yelled that the tug they were approaching was towing a barge. Their course was taking them between the two vessels. Turner liked their course. He didn't want to tack.

"Turner yelled at the bowman," Patsy says. "Is there slack in the towline? Can we sail over it?

"Maybe, the bowman says, but we don't know if it is sunk nine feet.

"Turner said we were continuing, that we'd either make it or he'd tell us to jump or duck as the wire crossed over the deck. There were lots of commands being shouted, a lot of loud arguing for ten minutes or so, when the bowman yells that the tug is backing down, that the skipper is understanding the situation of this crazy race boat about to sail over his wire-cable towline. We sail over the line with big cheers from our crew, the tug's blowing his horn, and Turner's yelling, Give that skipper a case of champagne! And we did, we got the tug's name and destination, got a case to him. He was delighted he could help. And he did, he helped us win the Lipton Cup."

Eagle won the SORC that year, upsetting the favorites (*Windward Passage* and *Ondine*) and winning five of the six races. Patsy stayed aboard for the Newport-to-Bermuda Race

In her working uniform, Patsy tweaks Eagle's *varnish prior to the Chicago-Mackinac Race, 1970.*

in June, for the Chicago-to-Mackinaw Race, and for a month of being trial horse for *Gretel*, the Australian challenger for the America's Cup ("*Eagle* was faster," she says. "Even in transatlantic conformation, with beat-up sails, *Eagle* was faster"). *Eagle* would win the World Ocean Racing Championship, the only boat in the competition with a woman in its working crew.

Patsy was doing some work in *Eagle's* cockpit one sunny afternoon in Newport, bikini-clad, when a photographer approached her about doing a shoot for *Playboy*. He left her his card. Rosie told her it was a bad idea. Patsy never called him back.

Patsy would leave *American Eagle* before the WORC honor was bestowed. David Steere, owner of *Yankee Girl*, had been impressed enough by Patsy's presence on board to offer her a well-paying job as manager of his new *Yankee Girl*, which was being completed at Palmer Johnson's yard in Sturgeon Bay, Wisconsin. It was convenient because of her relationship at the time with Mickey Spillane, who had been named captain of *Yankee Girl*. On Labor Day weekend 1970, she was scheduled to drive to Mamaroneck, New York, to pick up Spillane and drive with him to Sturgeon Bay. Car trouble had canceled that plan, causing Patsy to spend the weekend on a schooner named *Ululu*, where she met Bill Bolling.

Within a month after the Labor Day weekend cruise, Patsy and Bill were living together on *Ululu* with Bill's three cats. Eggemoggin had been joined by another Siamese, named Esther, after the famous swimming movie star Esther Williams, for whom Bill had done stunt work. Osa was the third cat, named after the woman pioneer explorer and filmmaker Osa Johnson, whose best-selling autobiography—*I Married Adventure*—had captivated him. Now, he was about to do the same thing.

"Bill's and my relationship was passionate," Patsy says, "wonderful, but also very scary. Bill was away for a couple weeks early on, delivering large powerboats. I had to take *Ululu* out for sea trials because she was for sale, and we were restoring *Lady Francis* by then, a seventy-five-foot shrimper. I had to have my head on a swivel no matter what I was doing in case Bill's wife might be coming down the dock." Bill's and Betty's relationship had long been ended, but she was still the wife.

For all his fondness for spontaneity, his random, headlong dash through life, his craft as a hustler when it came to doing business, and the deep well of winning charm he commanded, Bill Bolling was courteous, mannerly. The bells had rung for Bill Bolling. In Patsy he had met his match, as in ideal, or perhaps as perfect in terms of a relationship. As Patsy puts it, "Both our adventure glands were stuck wide open."

Patsy was also a match where capability was concerned. Bill knew the stories, the depth of her traditional seamanship, her car racing, the water-ski shows, her commendable status on *Eagle*, not to mention the wild SORC parties she hosted. Bolling was forty-two. His divorce was an impending formality. Patsy might have been dismissive about finding a partner who was "it," but Bill had different ideas.

"He asked me if I had told my parents about him," Patsy says. "I said no, I hadn't. He says, Well you better do it."

Patsy drove to Miami, picked up her father, and brought him to *Ululu* for dinner. Walking down the dock they ran into Bill on his way to the showers. He took her aside.

"You tell him yet?"

"No."

"Jesus, you just had forty minutes in the car with him!"

Patsy took Lou aboard. "He loved the schooner," Patsy says. "I gave him a tour. I'm cooking. He's on the settee.

I said, I have something to tell you. I'm living on this boat.

"Yeah."

"I'm living in the aft cabin."

"Yeah, you're running the boat, right?"

"Bill is in the aft cabin too."

"Ohhh, what's going on?"

"Bill and I are together."

Ululu, *"the love boat" where Patsy met Bill Bolling in 1970.*

"Oh my God, Jesus, Mary, and Joseph, oh Patsy, your life is just beginning and his is half over."

"Thanks a lot, Daddy."

"You're gonna have to tell your mother, because I'm not. What am I gonna do?"

"Not to worry, I'll tell her."

Patsy didn't see her mother until Christmas. Bill had sold *Ululu* by then. They had moved aboard *Lady Francis*, the seventy-five-foot trawler they were restoring, and Patsy had added an ocelot named Ozzie to their cat collection. Ozzie would turn out to be the Bollings' toughest pet: he was a biter. Bill suggested they take the family to the Bahamas on *Lady Francis* for the holidays. Off they went rigged for fun, with a Harley Sportster on the top deck, a sailing dinghy, and a Boston Whaler in davits.

"Mom greets us. I tell her I'm staying in the aft cabin with Bill. She exults, says she was wondering when this was going to happen. Wonderful, great news, she was so happy. She was always bringing men she'd met at the beach home to meet me."

Above: Charisma (Patrician), *Patsy and Bill restored and sold to Ted Kennedy.* **Opposite page:** *Ozzie the ocelot, and* **Lady Francis.**

Over a two-year period, Patsy and Bill would finish the *Lady Francis* project. They would survive the delivery of *Charisma* (*Patrician*), complete its restoration, and sell the boat to Ted Kennedy before they laid eyes on *Puritan*.

Raynell Smith, crew aboard Puritan, *shows off the artistic signage of her husband, Kaptain Krunch.*

VI

RESTORATION

There were many surprises as they started *Puritan*'s restoration. One was when they discovered a screw cap on the bottom surface of *Puritan*'s fourteen-foot-long steel rudder. The cap was so difficult to get off that Patsy and Bill assumed it hadn't been removed since 1931, when the boat had been built. Finally, using heat and various tools, they were able to remove the cap. A liquid began dripping out, what seemed to be an oil-and-water mix. Then they discovered another cap on the rudder's top surface. After hours' more application of heat and penetrating solvent, they got the cap to move. When they were able to remove it, liquid gushed from the bottom of the rudder.

Always game, Patsy stuck her finger into the flow and gingerly tasted it. Oil and water for sure, and the water was fresh. "They'd filled the rudder with oil," Patsy says, "because steel rusts from the inside out." Condensation will occur in an empty steel cavity thanks to temperature changes and the high moisture content of air in an underwater space. Condensation would promote rust. They power-washed the inside of the rudder the best they could and refilled it with light oil.

They also rediscovered chain lashing, a technique Patsy had learned from working on her father's old schooners. Chain lashing is a lengthy and tiresome job performed to remove rust from steel rigging. One takes a length of small, flexible chain (bicycle chain will do), passes it around the rusty shroud or stay, and saws it back and forth until the rust is removed. Chain lashing is followed by wire brushing. *Puritan*'s shrouds number eight for the mainmast, six for the foremast, each of them stretching upward for a minimum of fifty feet, not to mention numerous forestays, backstays, and the topmast rigging. Step three was to haul a crewman aloft again and lower him as he brushed linseed oil into the rigging. Step four was going aloft still again to rub white lead and tallow into the wires.

The dozen people Patsy and Bill had working on *Puritan* were a varied lot. They were either friends, relatives, acquaintances, or stragglers who happened along. Some of them had useful trades or some familiarity with boat work. Some didn't. One thing they had in common was wanting to be part of a team bringing a legendary vessel back to life. The possibility of being asked to crew on her when she sailed away was a tasty carrot dangling in the distance. And Bill's reputation was solid. Word on the dock was that he had three or four boats behind him, and that he did a decent job, treated his workers well.

From the outset Patsy and Bill ran a tight ship. It had to be. In the small River Bend Marina, with its narrow entrance and modest collection of boats forty feet and under, *Puritan* was in fact a major attraction. "Everybody and their dog were coming by," Patsy says. "People could see the mast from I-95. They had questions, wanted to talk. Bill made a sign: 'Talk to Bill ten cents a minute. Talk to Patsy five cents a minute. Crew no talk.'"

Workdays ran eight to five. Bill would arrive first with donuts and coffee and lay out the plan for the day. Sundays were off. "Sundays were always Bill's and my day at home," Patsy says. "Breakfast in bed. We might do a little work, like sewing baggy wrinkles for the rigging [lengths of soft, unlaid rope ends to prevent the sails from chafing] but we'd never go to the boat on a Sunday."

A man named Bob Stevens was an electrical engineer who had worked with Bill on previous boats. He was good with engines. They had an electronics guy, Lex Brinko, who had helped them move a Chesapeake bugeye Lou had bought on a whim, thinking it would make a good home for Pat and him (it didn't). A fellow named Albert had heard about the restoration on the waterfront grapevine and joined in. And one man, a parolee who had just been released from prison, sought them out saying he wanted to learn about boats. "Bill thought he might have been a plant to see if we were planning to move drugs," Patsy says. "But he turned out to be great, a nice guy, hard worker."

Bill's son Billy and a high school friend of his, Sherwood Michel, worked on the boat after school. After they'd sold *Ululu*, Bill and Patsy had moved into a rental house in Fort Lauderdale. Not long after they moved in, Billy's mother (Betty) sent him to live with his father. At the same time, thanks to age-related parental readjustments—the sale of boats (*Pike's Arm*) and changing living arrangements—Rosie also moved in with Patsy and Bill. That got them more workers after school, but having two uprooted sixteen-year-olds with lists of grievances did not make for a happy household.

"My parents had sold the house in Nassau, gotten rid of my horse and everything," Rosie says today. "They sent me to boarding school. I hated it but had to stay a year because Daddy couldn't get his deposit back. Then I left, but I didn't have a place to live, so they sent me to Patsy and Bill. I eventually ran away because it was a little bit passive-aggressive living there."

There was undoubtedly some of the old babysitting angst left over between Patsy and Rosie at that stage. They would grow out of it and become very close, especially when their middle sister, Gabrielle, began to fail. Rosie would later be amused to discover that Patsy was including a birth-control pill among Rosie's morning vitamins during that ill-fated live-in situation. "I figured if I were going to be the mother of a teenage girl in the 1960s," Patsy says, "I was going to make sure there were no babies."

Patsy's friend Olive joined the crew after being made redundant at Bahamas Air. Having lost her job, Olive had called Patsy in tears. Soon she was in Fort Lauderdale, cooking, taking over sandwich-making from Patsy, putting her skills as a seamstress to work on sails, and making covers for settees and cushions below deck. Patsy and Bill saw that she attended Le Cordon Bleu in England. She'd stay with *Puritan* as cook long after it changed hands.

Raynell Smith got involved because she and her husband, Steve, known as Kaptain Krunch, were living aboard their small skipjack schooner, *Jolly Roger*, in the River Bend Marina. Krunch, whose nickname had in fact come from a cereal box, observed the refit of *Puritan* going on and was itching to get involved. A former drafts-man for Douglas Aircraft who had retired after a motor-cycle accident, Krunch introduced himself to Patsy and Bill, letting them know he could do boat lettering, signs, graphics, and also wiring. He would become a valuable player. Steve Smith passed away in 2021. Raynell remem-bers the excitement caused by the big schooner. "Sailing adventure?" she says today. "Anything would have been better than teaching public high school."

She and Patsy didn't hit it off at first. "We had totally different backgrounds," Raynell says. "I had a master's degree in English from UVA. I'd been in academia for quite a while. That's not Patsy's world, and sailing wasn't my world.

"Patsy was like a guy," Raynell recalls. "So forceful. There were five men doing various jobs. She was directing all the projects. Not sure where Bill was, but Patsy seemed to be in charge. She had a thumb in every pie. The fuel tanks were being cleaned out. I remember Sherwood Mi-chel was in the tank scraping rust and shoveling out old fuel residue. He got sick doing it. Patsy was not the most sympathetic of people."

Patsy and Raynell are good friends today. But their initial encounter wasn't promising. "She was coming aboard as a stewardess to help Olive in the galley," Patsy says. "Part of that job is to clean toilets, make beds, do laundry. She asked where the rubber gloves were. I said, What gloves? She said she wasn't going to clean toilets without gloves on. I said, Well honey, forget that. It ain't hap'nin'. When she had time off she'd take a guest chair and put it wherever she wanted. I'd tell her to move, this area was for guests. She'd say there were no guests around. I'd say it didn't matter. She didn't know her place yet. I didn't want her on board. I was overruled. She was Kaptain Krunch's lady, and she learned quickly. She became a very good sailor."

"I learned there was a lot of Captain Lou in Patsy," Raynell says today. "She treated the crew like Lou treated his crew. We were slaves who had jobs to do. It was funny in a way. She really liked us, but we had to do certain things like 'real sailors' did them. Lou disowned his son, who didn't want to sail around on boats. He wanted a real job. Patsy became Lou's son. He dragged her around, taught her everything any sailor would need to know. She was more knowledgeable about sailing than Bill. Sometimes that was a matter of conflict."

After the boat was cleaned up enough, and the heads were working, a couple workers were allowed to stay on board. That was good for security. The on-boards had a microwave and a fridge, but no other cooking was allowed. "When girlfriends arrived," Patsy says, "they

Following pages: A beehive of hard, demanding work behind the six-month restoration of the badly debilitated Puritan.

got to eat and drink but they didn't get paid." Their job was to take every fixture off the boat below, every hinge, every knob, and clean and polish or paint them. "They'd sit on an old sail working until they got so tired they had to take a nap," Patsy says. "They were in their bikinis, keeping the boys happy."

In 2023, Billy's high school friend Sherwood Michel was captain of *Sorcha*, a 150-foot motor yacht. He went ocean racing at an early age, and became mate on the 12-meter *Heritage* when he was just twenty years old. When he was still in school, Sherwood's friendship with Billy led to working with Billy's father restoring boats. When *Puritan* came along, so did Michel.

"I took to their knowledge of boats like a sponge," Sherwood says today. "I knew I was going to make boats a career. I'd dropped out of college my third year. But *Puritan* was grand-scale, a massive, classic schooner that needed so much work. Where do you start? How do you do it?

"A lot of the professional side of me started with Patsy being very regimented. With that came clarity, black and white. Do it right, and do it the same way every time. Don't put the cart before the horse. The orderly fashion played well with me. Now I take a boat into a shipyard with my contractors, my people, my pay schedules all lined up, with my budget and time line organized. That information, that knowledge, came from a base Patsy and Bill provided. They were there to nurture you if you were interested. Not many were, like Bill's son, Billy. He dropped out."

The *Puritan* job didn't end well for Michel. After the restoration, during a charter in Jamaica, he and another crewman returned to the boat at 4:00 a.m. one morning quite drunk, and proceeded to bang on the piano and carry on. Bill fired him. "I took the whole shooting match," Michel says today. "It was me. Fine. What I did was inappropriate. Okay. Don't do that again. But I didn't burn my bridge. It was a onetime deal. I took the blame. Went on to make a fabulous career. I stayed in touch by writing postcards. When Bill's health failed, I went to see him."

Sherwood wasn't the only one working inside the tanks. Penny Parrot's son, Jody, was tabbed for scraping the rust off the inside of the water tanks. Why? Because at age nine he was small enough to fit into the opening.

"I would imagine it was Patsy who suggested me," Jody says. Jody is a yacht broker today, having followed in his mother's footsteps. "I remember climbing into the hole and getting handed a scraper, a hammer, and a wire brush and going at it. It was my first job away outside the family. I'm sure they paid me at least fifty cents an hour. I remember feeling honored to be part of the team. And it was a team. People were getting paid peanuts, like fifty dollars a week. They pulled it together with a team of hoodlums. Come work all day for the adventure and free peanut-butter-and-jelly sandwiches. Tuna fish on Fridays. Patsy is Catholic.

"My mother and Patsy were adventurous women, unique to their era. They took joy in proving to the world what everybody thought they couldn't do. And Patsy and Bill, they always seemed to have a blast together, showing the world how to live a real adventurous life. Part of their relationship was getting a rise out of the world by doing things most people wouldn't do. Couldn't do!

"As a kid I wondered about money between my family and Patsy and Bill. It was always a factor that neither of us had any money, we just looked like we did. And somehow we pulled it off. They had a Cadillac convertible and a hundred-foot schooner. When my mother bought *Royono*, it was either buy a house for eighteen thousand dollars or the boat for twenty-four thousand. She took a chance and bought the boat. Somehow we made it through.

"Patsy was like my aunt. Once she bet me I couldn't climb up to the first set of spreaders on *Royono*. We had a hundred-foot mast. The first spreaders were around forty feet up. I climbed up. Mom came home from work asking, Where's Jody. Patsy said, Why, he's up there.

"On that *Royono* delivery I used to serve Patsy her tea. She'd be lying naked on the foredeck. I'd bring her ice tea. It was brown liquid, anyway. Probably Mount Gay. As a kid I'm thinking, I can't wait to grow up and be like these guys."

Patsy and Bill divided the work. She had down below, Bill had the deck. The first thing they did was move all the spars ashore, including the main boom, which was forty-eight feet long. But then, Patsy says, "They did the caulking of the deck my way. We did end up using some silicon-type poop, but mainly we used hemp from Nova Scotia, then poured in sealant with linseed oil or something similar. Then the black rubber goo that was boiling on the dock. They'd come with a bucket and pour it on. We got it all over, had to take an eight-inch disc sander and do the whole deck afterward."

Back in her domain below deck, Patsy took on the job of de-rusting and painting the steel overhead deck frames. There were sixty-five of them on eighteen-inch centers, stretching athwartships (maximum beam of *Puritan* is twenty-three feet). A daunting job. She attacked the rust with a nibbler head in an electric drill. For painting, one of the guys came up with a spray rig, something she'd never used. "That was fun," she says, "spraying overhead with paint running down my arm. Bob Derecktor used to give us crap about tackling a hundred-foot schooner with one-inch putty knives. Using a spray gun was more like it."

Scott Campbell remembers Patsy taking on the spray-painting job. Campbell is a retired yacht captain today, with an impressive offshore resume thanks to Patsy getting him involved with Ted Turner and *American Eagle*. Campbell had been working with Bill restoring boats for two years before Patsy appeared on the scene.

"She was a tough cookie," he says of Patsy in those early *Puritan* days. "She was the boss. You didn't argue with her. Everything she did was a bit different, but she didn't care. In those days you didn't see women doing what she did at her level. She was forceful. People looked up to her. She was always right about everything. When she wasn't, well, she wasn't. But in her mind she was. We're about the same age, but I always thought of her as my mother."

The work list was comprehensive. Every nut and bolt, doorknob and latch was removed, cleaned, or replaced. All turnbuckles and davits were freed up, cleaned, and lubricated. One hundred thirty-seven blocks were taken apart, cleaned, stripped, oiled, and varnished with twelve coats. The engine room was scrubbed and painted. The main engine and generator were taken apart and rebuilt ashore. Engine sections had to be hoisted out through the galley hatch and swung over the rail into a dinghy, which was moved along the bulkhead to connect with a crane mounted on the back of a truck. A new galley was installed with built-in refrigeration, a deep freeze, and a double-oven propane stove. Where possible, rust on the interior hull was attacked with a nibbler, abluted with Ospho, red-leaded, then painted.

The topsides were ground down and painted on the port side and half of the starboard side. "The other half was against the dock," Patsy says. "We painted from a canoe, a small dinghy, and a raft Bill built. Some of the plating had to be cut out and replaced, and there was deterioration under the portholes. Those areas had to be cut out with new metal welded in place, covered with red lead, then painted white. We made the portholes workable, and designed wind scoops for them for use in port.

"The deckhouse windows and frames—and no two were alike—were removed and rebuilt by our carpenter, Don Donley. And we added a new navigation system including radar, VHF, high-seas radio, AM radio, and an Omega nav system."

New sails arrived: forestaysail, flying jib, and mainsail.

After twenty-one thousand man hours and $128,000 spent (around $900,000 in 2024 dollars), *Puritan's* face had been properly lifted. With the restoration nearing the end, co-owner and backer from heaven Gerald Gidwitz asked if his wife, Jane, might have a hand in decorating the main salon. Gidwitz had been a frequent visitor to the restoration of "his boat," but had not participated other than financially. "We said, Go for it, absolutely," Patsy says. Meanwhile, Olive had made up some temporary tan covers just to protect everything.

Measurements were taken and sent to Jane Gidwitz, who selected the material and went over the job with her professional seamstress. A few weeks later, the covers arrived. "I almost puked, they were so bad," Patsy says. "Diamonds and stripes, black, brown, and white. We put them on, then covered the settees with sheets so we didn't have to look at them."

On July 4, 1973, roughly six months after the work had begun, and after a week of testing all systems, *Puritan* was prepped for its first sail. Just a day sail. Thirty or forty people were invited, including the crew from River Bend Marina and the Gidwitzes. "Jane had never seen the boat," Patsy says. "She was very enthusiastic, loved everything about it until she walked below into the main cabin. She was horrified: Oh my goodness, she said, what a travesty! We can't use them—look at that settee! I told her it was what she had sent. I know, she said, but it's *awful*!!

"Gerald laughed. He knew. Olive quickly got the tan covers and put them on. Jane was a lovely lady."

An advertisement, with the dotted line showing
charterers the areas **Puritan** *would be cruising.*

VII

SHOWING THE FLAG

The same energy and commitment that had gone into the restoration drove the selling of *Puritan*. "Our philosophy was to show the boat by using it, keeping it moving," Patsy says. "Show that it works and people are having fun on it instead of having buyers coming around to see it sitting idle at a dock gathering dust."

One might think that after such a difficult, hard-won, emotional affair with *Puritan*, Patsy and Bill would have wanted to take pride in ownership. But the hefty maintenance of the large schooner wasn't in their budget, and Gidwitz's seagoing fling was taking other directions. Moreover, despite their love of boats, boats were their business. The transient nature of it went along with their

adventure-driven lives: use it up, get more. Even if ownership had been affordable, the majestic *Puritan* wouldn't
have been enough to keep them engaged.

During a shakedown cruise to the Bahamas, the crew
put the vessel aground to finish bottom work. Driving a
hundred-ton schooner onto the sand in such a way that
the boat will stay upright when the tide ebbs and will refloat when the tide floods is an outrageous but workable
notion that takes considerable skill. Before railways and
travel lifts, it was the usual way to do bottom work. After
a good scrubbing, the vessel headed north to take advantage of summer activity.

The end of July 1973 found *Puritan* starring at the
Annapolis Boat Show, where the old girl won the antique
yacht parade. Then she visited Maryland's Eastern Shore
before spending a few days in New York. Then she was
off to Newport, Rhode Island, Patsy having organized a
photo shoot to be done along the way by *Motor Boating &
Sailing* magazine. The breeze had come up, making photographer Pete Smyth happy. *Puritan* was on the cover of
the December 1973 issue. The story: "A Queen Is Reborn."

They sailed to Nova Scotia and up the LaHave River
for Patsy's birthday in August of 1973. There was surely
some pride in that. They hauled out in Lunenburg to do a
proper bottom job, using the yard's high-pressure rams to
try and release the centerboard. It wouldn't budge. Sailing
upwind without a centerboard (or extended keel) causes
a sailing vessel to make almost as much progress sideways
as forward. It was a handicap further plaguing *Puritan*'s
crew when they returned to Newport. Their dock neighbor was *America*, a replica of the vessel that had beaten a

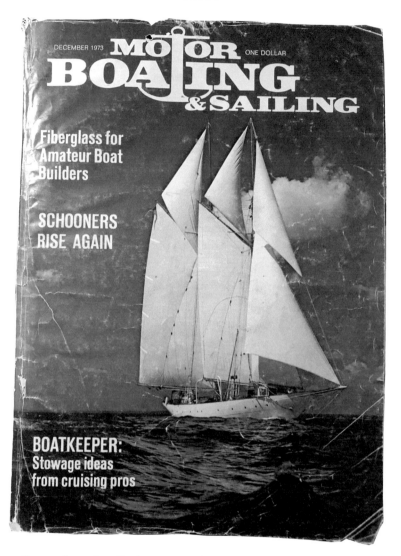

DECEMBER 1973 ONE DOLLAR

MOTOR BOATING &SAILING

Fiberglass for Amateur Boat Builders

SCHOONERS RISE AGAIN

BOATKEEPER: Stowage ideas from cruising pros

fleet of England's fastest yachts around the Isle of Wight in 1851, winning a trophy named after her—the America's Cup—and starting an international contest that is the oldest ongoing event in sports.

America's crew was keen to have a race with *Puritan*. The specifications of the two yachts are quite similar, but

America was ten feet longer on the waterline, and displaced ten fewer tons. *Puritan* carried more sail, and was deeper by three feet with the centerboard down. But the centerboard wouldn't move. They all knew that without a board to ensure the boat's upwind performance, it would be pointless to have a race. "We told them we'd love to race," Patsy says today, "but only if we could get our board down."

A race between the two legendary yachts, even if *Puritan* lost to the swift *America*, would generate great publicity. They had to try moving the board one more time. They lowered their main anchor, a three-hundred-pounder, hooked it to a halyard, and guided it aft until it was alongside the centerboard. Fortunately, there was a ring welded on the exposed bottom surface of the board. The anchor was lowered. Divers attached the anchor to the ring at low tide and snugged it up close with a come-along. As the tide rose, the three-hundred-pound weight would be hanging from the centerboard.

They waited. For three days the tide ebbed and flooded. Nothing. "Day four we were sitting below having lunch," Patsy says, "when all the sudden the goddamn ship shuddered, the plates were chattering in the galley, the rigging was shaking, and Bill says, There goes the centerboard. The boys jumped over, and sure enough it was down. It was one amazing mess of rust and awfuls, barnacles and tons of mud. We cleaned it, wire brushed it, poured oil down the chain hoist and cranked it up and down many times. We sent a nice calligraphed note to *America* saying we were ready to race."

The two crews had a skipper's meeting, agreed on a course to sail, and the gun went off. The wind was ten to twelve knots, light for hundred-ton schooners. The first mark was downwind, followed by an upwind leg back to the finish. In addition to the regular crews, both boats had a dozen guests on board who were attending a Rolls-Royce Owners' Club meeting. "We had a good start," says Patsy, who was driving, "but *America* was coming on, charging. She was fast, a lot faster than us. We were desperate. We had a huge gennaker up. We even had a Laser sail lashed to the gallows behind the helm. We were doing eight, nine knots. But *America* went by us and was leaving us with her gollywobbler up" (a large, quadrilateral reaching sail set between a schooner's two masts).

The gollywobbler was *America*'s undoing. As the boat approached the mark, the crew couldn't get the sail down. *Puritan* turned inside the famous black schooner, rounded the mark, lowered its centerboard to its full fourteen feet eight inches, trimmed sails, and headed for the finish. Behind them, *America* had finally gotten the troublesome sail down and was gaining. The start/finish line was the Claiborne Pell/Newport Bridge. "She was coming on," Patsy says, "but there wasn't enough runway. We beat *America*, fired our cannon the second our bow-sprit passed under the bridge so there was no doubt about it. Later we learned none of the guests got fed on *America*. Olive had served a delightful lunch onboard *Puritan*."

Perhaps spurred on by that unlikely victory, they sailed *Puritan* west to Mystic Seaport Museum and entered the Seaport's annual schooner race, winning again. Another trophy added glitz to their next stop, which was Electric Boat Company, ten miles down the coast from Mystic, where *Puritan* had been built

Puritan *(above) after crossing the finish line under the Newport Bridge ahead of* America. *Bill Bolling (below) at* Puritan's *helm after the finish.*

in 1931. To Patsy and Bill's amazement, they were snubbed by the famous builder of submarines.

"We had written letters to them saying we'd stop by," Patsy says, "and their response had been unenthusiastic. But we dropped the hook out front anyway and Bill went in, invited them all out for cocktails. Three people showed up, workers, not one high mucky-muck. One man who came out said it was his grandfather who had built *Puritan*'s knotty-pine interior with matching panels. He gave us a photo of the boat he'd stolen off the wall of the main office, saying they didn't give a shit. Imagine, the only yacht they ever built, a job that saved their butts when government contracts were slow, and they didn't bother to come out."

While Electric Boat wasn't impressed, *Puritan*'s well-scripted showing of the flag turned out to be good for business. Several buyers were nibbling at the boat's listing. But first, Bill had something more important in mind.

"In 1973 Bill said, We need to get married," Patsy recalls. "I said, Is there any reason to get married? And he said, Yes. We're chartering to fancy people and we're living in the deckhouse together. It isn't right. He didn't get on his knee and offer me a fabulous ring or anything loving. He said, We need to get married. But that was Bill.

"Our relationship was romantic. He went for a walk every morning, and every morning he would bring me a flower he'd picked along the way. We got married because we wanted one another totally. He was forty-two when we met in 1970. I was twenty-eight. He said he was done looking. He used to tell people, 'Look at what I married. She can be wrenching a car, changing an engine, varnishing mahogany or greasing winches all day, then put on a ball gown and go dancing, looking like a million bucks.' He'd been to the jeweler for a wedding ring.

"He said, How 'bout we go to Barbados and get married in the Ocean View Hotel, same hotel, same room where your parents got married. So we did. I had to fill out the paperwork. At the time a woman had to choose one of three categories: divorced, widowed, or spinster. I said I wanted 'pleasure seeker,' but they wouldn't let me. At thirty years old I registered as a spinster. It was just us. No family."

No honeymoon either. Business called. The Bollings had booked a charter from a family who had rented a villa on the Jamaican waterfront for six weeks. They wanted *Puritan* standing by to take them for day sails. It was a cushy charter, not to be missed. Bill rounded up the crew, which included Olive, the cook; Scott Campbell; Kaptain Krunch and Raynell; and Sherwood Michel. Patsy wasn't on board. She had stayed home to interview new crew members and help secure more charters.

To improve their business, Bill had designated an area from the Bahamas to Jamaica he wanted to cruise. The idea was to sell it in packages. He drew up the proposal, gave it to brokers, and ran it as an advertisement in yachting magazines. Patsy had to be on hand to answer calls and take reservations. "Plus," as she says, "we had an ocelot in the backyard." The Bollings' many pets would eventually include two large Florida panthers (cougars), but Patsy says the ocelot was toughest of all to manage.

Puritan left Fort Lauderdale mid-December 1973. The course would take the boat around the east end of Cuba, through the Windward Passage separating Cuba and Haiti, and south to Jamaica. As they approached the passage, which could typically present rough going, there was a nasty fuel spill on board. At the time, *Puritan* had a 150-gallon "day tank" that fed the engine and generator. The 1,500-gallon main fuel tank refilled the day tank by electric pump. The temporary engineer Bill had hired for the delivery to Jamaica had mistakenly left the pump on, overfilling the day tank (which was in the galley), rupturing the interior baffle and bursting a connection. Oily, smelly diesel fuel was everywhere. Bill was livid. The fuel had to be cleaned up immediately and the line to the engine restored. Priming a big diesel is a tricky job. But the work couldn't be done with *Puritan* on a heel, sailing to windward in fifteen to eighteen knots of wind.

A few miles dead ahead was the Bay of Mole (Bahie du Môle) on the northwest tip of Haiti, and the town of Môle Saint-Nicolas, where the guidebook suggested that parts to repair the fuel line might be available. The bay would offer protection from the wind, a calm anchorage where they could get to work. They thought.

No sooner had the crew dropped anchor than two large skiffs propelled by oars approached *Puritan*. Five men were in each skiff. As they got closer, the crew noticed that the visitors were small in stature. Several of them were wearing makeshift uniforms and carrying weapons. Scott Campbell, an ex-Marine, recognized M1 rifles and .45 caliber handguns. Assuming they were customs officers, Bill allowed them on board. Annoyed that the skiffs had begun bumping up against Puritan's hull, he ordered fenders to be deployed.

Language was an immediate problem. The Haitian French patois being spoken by the visitors was foreign to everyone on the crew except a young French-speaking hand named Kim, who could make some sense of it. With his help, and plenty of sign language, the message from the Haitians became clear: they wanted everyone off the boat.

"They were very curt, disrespectful to everyone," Scott Campbell recalls. "They were a sorry-looking bunch, like they didn't have a pot to piss in or a window to throw it out of."

"Bill said, No way, we're absolutely not getting off the boat," Raynell recalls. "The Haitians knew he was in charge because he was wearing a uniform. He had put it on when he saw them coming, brass buttons and gold stripes, epaulets—you'd laugh, but it looked official. He knew a uniform meant a lot to the Haitians. And there was nothing reticent about Bill. He had a commanding presence. If we'd left the boat he knew they would have picked it clean."

Bill was conflicted. He didn't want to leave the bay. There was work to be done, and the Windward Passage was kicking up. It was rough out there. In the confusion, Bill had managed to slip below and get some calls out to Patsy and to the Navy base in Guantanamo. They alerted a cruise ship and a military vessel, but both were many hours away. Meanwhile Patsy was making calls to the US Embassy and to the US Consulate in Haiti.

Negotiations with the Haitian militia went on. Bill Bolling not only had a commanding presence. He was a rapid-fire talker who was rarely at a loss for something to say. Angry Bolling could be scary. But usually Bill's delivery, whether critical or commending, was lighthearted, friendly, like he was definitely planning to buy the next round. The fact that the Haitians hardly understood a word of what he was saying, even with the prompting of deckhand Kim, simply helped Bill's effort to keep them at bay. It also allowed Bill and the crew to make plans without the Haitians knowing what was being said.

According to Raynell, no weapons were brandished. "We thought it was possible that one Haitian might have had a gun with bullets in it," she says. "But they really were a sorry-looking lot." And none of the *Puritan* crew was manhandled by the Haitians. "It was a hairy few hours," Scott says. "If it had gotten rough, I told Sherwood that I could take out any one of these little guys in a heartbeat. But it would be very quick, and he and Krunch would have to come in fast behind me. All three of us were big guys."

As it happened, no such heroic action was necessary. The negotiations, with both sides shouting and gesturing, moved on to the anchor. The Haitians had made it clear they wanted the boat moved closer to the village. By now, Bill understood that getting out of there was the priority, and that if they got any closer the whole village would likely be coming aboard to strip *Puritan* clean. Both sides wanted the anchor up. Bill let them know it would have to be done by hand, since both engine and generator were down.

The Haitians helped pull up the anchor, while the *Puritan* crew made sure it slipped back occasionally. Timing was important. The crew knew the offshore breeze would turn the schooner out to sea. They wanted sails raised before the anchor was off the bottom. Raising sails on *Puritan* took muscle, and time. It required several crew lining up on the halyards and pulling together. To hoist *Puritan*'s full complement of seven sails could take forty-five minutes.

Creating confusion was essential. Bill ran around barking orders and telling the Haitians to stand clear. As the anchor was being lifted, the crew raised the forestays'l, knowing a sail far forward would turn the bow away from the village toward open ocean. The foresail was also raised. When the anchor cleared the bottom, the forestays'l was trimmed, causing the boat to slowly turn seaward. A hundred-ton schooner doesn't accelerate very fast, but when *Puritan* began to build momentum there was panic among the Haitian militia.

"Bill shrugged, told them we couldn't stop the boat," Raynell says. "For them to sail away from Haiti on an American boat would not be good. There was lots of arguing and shouting, threats, but very soon they started throwing their guns into their skiffs, jumping in after them, and casting off. That was that. No way were they going to catch us with rowboats."

Two days later, *Puritan* arrived in Montego Bay, got the fuel spill cleaned up and the engine and generator reconnected and reprimed. Patsy flew in and joined the crew. The six-week charter went off as planned, uneventful except for Patsy insisting on firing the vessel's cannon at the stroke of midnight after a New Year's Eve dinner and many drinks ashore. In her enthusiasm she forgot to put the cannon on its lift to raise the barrel above the cap rail. "The blackened and splintered cap rail was rebuilt in the morning, by me," Patsy says, "with sawdust and epoxy until a dutchman could be scarfed in place."

The rest of the winter season was filled with charters in Jamaica, Grand Cayman, and finally in Cozumel, an island off the Yucatan coast of Mexico. The last was booked by Vernon Gray, the grandson of *Puritan*'s original owner, Edward W. Brown, who had passed away two weeks short of one year after his boat had been launched. Gray did not sail on *Puritan* as a child, but he grew up fascinated by his great-grandfather Vernon Brown's business as both broker and owner of clipper ships in Boston in the 1830s. Vernon Brown would become the first American head of Cunard Line. Gray is an avid sailor who cruised on a New York 40, raced an International One Design, and (at ninety years old) was sailing a thirty-eight-footer out of Mount Desert, Maine. Gray is a self-appointed family historian whose house in Vermont is a museum of nautical artifacts. An entire room is devoted to *Puritan*. Gray's handsomely illustrated book, *The Maritime History of the Vernon H. Brown Family*, covers more than two centuries of maritime endeavor. In 1973, when Gray saw *Puritan* on the cover of *Motor Boating & Sailing*, he picked up the telephone.

"The article made me aware the schooner was alive and well," Vernon Gray says today. "Patsy and Bill had won a schooner race in Mystic. I chartered the boat with two other couples."

In the '70s, Cozumel didn't have much in the way of marine services. *Puritan* needed fuel and water. Patsy and Bill talked a waterfront-restaurant owner into letting them use his water to fill their tanks. The only way to get close enough was to go bow in, putting *Puritan's* bowsprit across the restaurant's porch and into the dining room. "There was a bit of a sea," Patsy recalls. "In the rise and fall the bowsprit would almost hit the ceiling. But he let us do it. We said we'd buy lunch for everyone if he let us bring a fuel truck into his lot. He agreed."

"We sailed for a week and had a wonderful time," Vernon Gray says. "We did what most charterers don't do.

We sailed the boat hard in twenty-knot winds. We sailed to Isla Mujeres, off Cancun. It hadn't been developed. Went diving in a school of a thousand fish. It was memorable. We sailed like crazy.

"No one knows that boat better than Patsy," Gray says. "She knows how to set sails and steer, of course, but she also knows the plumbing, the galley, and the engine."

******

The brokers were juggling several offers to buy *Puritan*. The crew took the boat to Key West for work while negotiations proceeded. "Just a fluff," Patsy says. "We sanded the masts and brushed linseed on them, got the varnish done, cleaned the decks with oxalic acid, polished the rigging, cleaned the topsides. I got in the water to paint the boot. Gave the sails a wash. Because we were headed for Lauderdale and there were three possible buyers. We wanted her to look like new."

Annoyed at the casual attitude of the potential buyers, Bill had an old friend at Metro-Goldwyn-Mayer in Los Angeles send him a telegram saying the studio wanted to buy or charter *Puritan* for a movie for six months, must know immediately, please respond ASAP with decision because contracts are being signed—"just to get these people off their asses," Patsy says. Bill copied the brokers.

"The price was going up," Patsy says, "three hundred twenty-five thousand, three fifty, three seventy-five" ($2.25 to $2.56 million in 2024 dollars). "Negotiations went on for weeks. We agreed to the highest, which was a poor decision because we didn't get the money for weeks."

The buyer, an Austrian, sent his crew over to learn the ropes. The Bollings wouldn't let them live on the boat because the sale wasn't final. Taking a page from one of Lou Kenedy's favorite gambits, they began charging the buyer $300 a day demurrage, compensation for detaining a ship. "We were tied to the dock," Patsy says, "paying the bills, paying the crew, paying, paying. The transaction was done in May, the money didn't arrive until July. We didn't let the boat go until the check cleared."

With a new crew of ten onboard, including Olive, who was retained as cook, *Puritan* left Fort Lauderdale to cross the Atlantic. Their first day out, the bowsprit cracked and split, forcing *Puritan* back to Florida for repairs. "Probably too much sail," Patsy says.

Gerald Gidwitz was generous to the end. He took his cost of the restoration off the top, and split the balance with Patsy and Bill. But his continuing enthusiasm for boating was presenting a problem. "That was so much fun," Gidwitz had said the day the sale closed, "let's do it again, only with a bigger one." Thanks to charters, *Puritan* hadn't been available to him all the time. Before *Puritan* was sold, Gidwitz had bought another boat for himself. It was called *Jubilee*, a vintage seventy-two-foot Sparkman & Stephens racing yawl. "Gerald let us know he was wishing—hoping—we'd take it over and run it for him," Patsy says. "Not really run it, he had a good crew on board, but oversee it, keep an eye on it. We loved Gerald. He was a gentleman, a man of his word. He was a neat guy. But overseeing the boat, which by the way he kept on the Great Lakes in the summer, and keeping tabs on the crew, would have been too much. We were tired of freaking crew. There were always money problems, behavior problems, girlfriend problems."

Picaroon, *the 40-foot Stadel trawler the Bollings downsized to after an extended, taxing period.*

VIII

PAUSE

In truth, the Bollings needed a break. The prepping of *Ululu* for sale; the rigorous winter trip from the Great Lakes to Florida with *Charisma*; finishing and selling *Lady Francis* (the trawler); and restoring and selling *Puritan*—not to mention the frenzy of a passionate and complicated relationship along the way—had been enough to exhaust even Patsy and Bill. They left their rental in Fort Lauderdale and moved onto a trawler named *Picaroon*.

"We downsized," Patsy says. "From one hundred two feet to forty feet. We loved it. We parked at whatever friend's dock would have us, or anchored out. We went diving every day, spent summers cruising the Chesapeake, and winters in the Bahamas." Their share of the sale of *Puritan* had brought them a certain amount of financial comfort. They increased an existing investment in Mexican pesos, and took on little jobs like the occasional delivery, which paid the rent.

In 1975, responding to a tip about the Mexican peso being overvalued, they pulled out and bought silver from the Swiss Bank Leu, for four dollars and change per ounce. Headquartered (since 1775) in Zurich, Bank Leu had a branch in Nassau at the time. "Silver buyers had to have a secret name," Patsy says. "Bill was Captain Midnight. But when we'd go to the Nassau branch, I knew a bunch of the women working there. They'd say, Hey Patsy, haven't seen you in ages. Busted."

Bill's mother passed away that year. The lawyers' messages were friendlier than when his father had died, but complicated with trusts and bank ownership of a summer cottage on Lake Michigan. They spent several summers in the Michigan house while the web of trusts, bonds, and stocks were getting untangled. It turned out that in order to sell the cottage, first they had to buy it from the bank. "I think Bill cleared maybe around fifty thousand dollars from his mother's estate," Patsy says. "After the legal fees and other expenses were paid, I remember seeing a final check for four dollars and ninety-eight cents."

Boat restoration went on. In 1977 they bought *Pez Espada* ("swordfish," in English*)*, a handsome eighty-six-foot Mathis/Trumpy motor sailor. So much for downsizing. *Pez* was an elegant, spacious vessel that had been built for Eugene du Pont, first head of the modern-day DuPont corporation. He had named it *Morning Star*. Another former owner had been Paul Mantz, the intrepid

Opposite page: Pez Espada, *a Mathis/Trumpy 86-foot motor sailor.*

Hollywood stunt pilot who had died while filming *The Flight of the Phoenix*. It was Mantz who had changed the boat's name. Patsy and Bill lived aboard *Picaroon* while working on the motor sailor. When *Pez* was finished, they moved aboard after selling *Picaroon*. "We kept the name *Pez Espada*," Patsy says. "It was carved into the transom, making it easy to paint."

In the America's Cup match, 1885, **Puritan (USA) leads challenger Genesta (GBR). Painting by James E. Buttersworth.**

In the summer of 1979, they traded *Pez Espada* for *Jaru*, another classic "gold-plater," a seventy-five-foot motor yacht by Trumpy. It was a trade, plus $100,000 for the Bollings. For a change, one of their acquisitions was in good shape. "*Jaru* didn't need much," Patsy says. "Just a facelift, a fluffing. She had the Edward Fields sculptured carpet, and beautiful fixtures, lots of chrome, and flashy stuff. We had the Buttersworth painting we'd gotten from my father hanging in the saloon. Let's say we weren't in our tacky mode. We kept her fancy. We went to Abaco and did the topsides, the varnish, cleaned the engine room." *Jaru* also had a twenty-two-foot North American runabout, which was handy for spearfishing on the reefs, or visiting islands with no accommodations for the big boat.

Once while motoring back from the Bahamas to Fort Lauderdale on *Jaru*, the North American had broken loose. "We never would have known," Patsy says. "The runabout was under tow a hundred feet back and the bridge on *Jaru* was far forward. But when the towrope broke, the shackle got launched like an arrow and embedded itself in the transom with the crack of a rifle shot." It was rough going. *Jaru* was rolling along at six knots in quartering seas. "The cats were all sick," Patsy recalls. The runabout had been alternately surfing toward *Jaru* and being jerked hard as *Jaru* rolled down each wave. The towline had finally parted.

Bill turned the boat and got close to the runabout, putting it in *Jaru*'s lee. "I told Bill, You drive, and I jumped over with my life jacket in one hand and the keys to the boat in my mouth. I got in the boat, no problem because we kept the outdrive down to create drag and keep the runabout pointed at us. It made a handy step. The boat started right up, thank heaven. I drove it close to *Jaru*, in the big boat's lee, then jumped over to tie the new line onto the ring bolted into the boat's stem. I realized I'd left the life jacket in the runabout."

With the runabout secure, Patsy had to get back aboard *Jaru*. Bill had dropped a floppy Jacob's ladder over the side for her. "Those things are no fucking good for anything," Patsy says, "a useless piece of shit. I'm wobbling up the ladder with *Jaru* pitching and rolling, in my wet clothes, cold, beat up. I get aboard and Bill says, I'm so glad you're back, it's time for lunch."

It was a good summer until Hurricane David swept through the Bahamas. At the time it was the most intense hurricane ever to make landfall on the East Coast of the United States. David was a Category 5 storm reaching peak sustained winds of 175 miles per hour, causing massive loss of life in Dominican Republic, and more than two thousand deaths in all. Damage from David exceeded $1.5 billion.

When they heard about David, the Bollings made a fast track to Man-O-War Cay, a thin, mile-long strip of an island five miles east of Abaco and 150 miles east of West Palm Beach, Florida. Nothing is east of Man-O-War but Western Sahara, Africa, after crossing 3,500 miles of ocean. But the Bollings knew Man-O-War, knew of a little protected "hurricane hole" of a basin more suited to dinghies than seventy-five-foot motor yachts. With the runabout lashed alongside to serve as extra power (bow thruster, hip thruster), they pushed through the cut, put out two anchors, and kept the engines turning over just in case. "There was no sea in the little basin," Patsy recalls, "but we couldn't open the door from pilothouse to deck because the wind was so strong. The big problem was the fucking coconuts flying. The whole bridge of the boat was glass. Some of the windows had vinyl coverings. The wind was tearing the coconuts off the trees and launching them at a hundred and fifty miles an hour." The topsides took several hits, but all the glass, and the Bollings, survived.

The price of silver was climbing. It would close at the end of 1979 at $32.20 an ounce, nearly eight times what the Bollings had paid for it. They decided it was time to cash in. "Bank Leu in Zurich would be closed over the holidays," Patsy says, "so we decided to be standing on their doorstep when they opened again on January 2."

Feeling flush, they flew on the Concorde to Paris, arriving at 6:00 a.m. Paris time. They hired a taxi with an English-speaking driver for the day, visiting several of the best attractions and hosting their driver for lunch. They made the 4:00 p.m. plane to Zurich. As planned, they were at the door when Bank Leu opened the day after New Year's. "Silver was thirty-something dollars," Patsy says. "We wanted to sell it all, but the banker talked us into selling only half of it. We took a wad and went skiing at Klosters, got a fancy hotel room and hired an instructor for a week. When we got back to Zurich, silver had dropped into the twenties, and we were some pissed at the banker. But we left the rest in. Silver went crazy, topping out near fifty-three dollars an ounce. That's when the Hunt brothers were manipulating the silver market. We rode it down, lived on it till it was gone."

Time to get more.

For two years they had stayed in Fort Lauderdale, boat-brokerage central, while trying to sell *Jaru*. They were even living at a broker's house, paying him $500 a month dockage, and doing small charter jobs like evening cocktail cruises. *Jaru* was a tough sell. The original owner had specified only two main cabins, feeling that guests should have the same space as the owner. "She

was squeaky clean," Patsy says of the boat, "and one of the prettier Trumpy's ever built, but the lack of accommodations was killing us. We showed her many, many times. We were sick of living on it. You needed a varnish sprinkler to keep it up."

Newport was alive with activity in 1982. Preparation for the 1983 America's Cup match was in full swing. Luxury cruisers like *Jaru* were in demand as spectator boats. Figuring it was a great place to show the flag, that spring Patsy and Bill made the 1,200-mile trip to Newport in ten days. It was an expensive trip in a vessel like *Jaru*, cruising at ten knots with twin three-hundred-horsepower diesels gulping down eight to ten gallons an hour. As expected, charters came easily for watching the 12-meter yachts scrimmaging. *Jaru* cruised tony Nantucket and Martha's Vineyard, and made the Newport Boat Show. But no buyers appeared.

Their life changed when they got a call from Dick Bradley. "Come to Para-dyze," he said, and they did.

The airport light project was an example of the Bollings' extra-curricular enthusiasm.

IX

THE FARO BLANCO RAT PACK

They'd met Dick Bradley along the way.

The boating subculture is divided geographically into sizable neighborhoods. One generally keeps up with boats, people, and activity in whichever body of water one happens to be floating. The East Coast of the United States has two major boating centers: Annapolis, Maryland, and Newport, Rhode Island. Florida has Fort Lauderdale on the East Coast, and St. Petersburg on the West. The Caribbean has Nassau and Antigua. Then there are the Great Lakes; the Gulf of Mexico; San Diego and south; Newport (California); greater Los Angeles; San Francisco Bay; and greater Seattle.

People like the late Dick Bradley, a columnist for *Motor Boating & Sailing* who wrote about living with his wife, Dory, aboard their fifty-five-foot Huckins Fairform Flyer (designed and built by the company that made PT boats during the war), were notable for their bridging of several neighborhoods. Bradley, like the Bollings for their well-publicized boating restorations, was something of a celebrity among the marine crowd.

The two couples had met in Fort Lauderdale, when the Bollings were trying to sell *Jaru* and the Bradleys

Dick Bradley, a live-aboard yachting writer, made Jim Kelsey an offer he couldn't refuse.

were parked at a motel with a dock. They had gotten along so well that Patsy and Bill had painted Bradley's boat. They found out he was going to borrow $5,000 to have the hull painted. "We said, Hell no," Patsy says. "Feed us and we'll do it." With a dinghy and a painting barge, and two people to a side, they did it in four days. "The first day we sanded the hull and wiped her down,"

Patsy says. "Day two we undercoated. Next morning we light-sanded and undercoated again for a good base. Day four we light-sanded and painted a finish coat all day, doing one side, then the other, then the first side again when it was dry." The cost of food and rum was up there, but nowhere near $5,000.

With his boat sparkling off-white, Dick Bradley set a course for Marathon, Florida, and the Faro Blanco Mari-

Patsy and Jim Kelsey with his 1934 Oldsmobile powered by a Corvette engine.

na that he'd heard had just changed hands. Faro Blanco's new owner was Jim Kelsey, who had a successful career behind him in motor sports. Kelsey is a fit, quietly confident man with an elaborate mustache. He's a hot-rod guy, a sheet-metal genius who can start with a basic car shape he likes (the unwritten rule is from 1949 or before), and restyle and rebuild it into an eye-catching automotive creation called a street rod. He built his first car when he was fourteen. His first business was a body shop in Connecticut, where he became sought-after for his paint work. He's particularly proud of one hot rod he built: *The Fly*. It made the cover of *Hot Rod Deluxe* magazine. "*Fly* was a '34 Ford

Roadster," Kelsey says, "a highboy, open wheel, Cadillac engine, laid-back windshield, and custom grill."

In 1980, Kelsey, his wife, Christa, and their three-month-old infant were on vacation in Key West, Florida, staying with friends, going boating, fishing, and enjoying the Keys' laid-back style. Like many visitors, they said they didn't want to go back north. Unlike most visitors, they really meant it, and started looking for property.

For fun, a real estate agent showed them Faro Blanco Marina, facing the Gulf of Mexico on the west end of Marathon. The $3.5-million price tag was way out of their league. But Jim thought about it all the way home. He called the agent, who told him that the owners would agree to hold the paper and the down payment was around half a million. Jim was on the next plane back.

"I remember driving into Faro Blanco and thinking, Holy crap, what is this place," Kelsey says. "There was a band playing with a good-looking lead singer, blonde, with large breasts if I remember correctly, singing a song I'd never heard before: Jimmy Buffett's *Why Don't We Get Drunk (And Screw).* The cars lined up were Mercedes and Jaguars. There were big yachts everywhere, the palm trees were waving in the breeze, the swimming pool was an eyeful. I looked at the agent and said, Sold!"

The Kelseys hit it off with the owners, Eric and Susan Ball. "Eric asked me what I was going to sell to buy the place, and I said everything I own, including the cars. He asked what cars. Two Cobra replicas I had built, and a Pantera. Eric said he'd take all three as part of the down payment."

Kelsey had just bought a ninety-seven-slip marina for 3.5 million bucks and was wondering what the hell he had done, how he was going to make it work, when here came Dick Bradley pulling into the marina in his Huckins. "He introduces himself," Kelsey recalls, "says he's a writer for *Motor Boating & Sailing.* I was supposed to know who he was, but I had no clue. He said he wrote a monthly column about living aboard and he'd like to do it from my marina. I said, Okay, great, that's wonderful. He says he knows everyone in the boating world, and he'll teach me how it works. Then he says he makes $1,800 a month for his column, and he could live on that if I could provide free food, a car to drive, and a free slip.

"I couldn't say yes fast enough," Kelsey says. "I knew nothing about boating. I needed to find out, or fail. I'd been in a lot of hot-rod magazine articles, so I knew how important magazine promotion of anything was in those days. Articles were like free advertising. The deal with Bradley turned out to be the smartest thing I ever did."

Bradley's first call was to the Bollings. The timing was right. They were sick of Fort Lauderdale and needed to change their luck. "Two weeks after Bradley had moved in," Jim Kelsey says, "he tells me the Bollings are coming, great people, high on the list of people everyone likes. They pulled in on *Jaru*, this gorgeous 1964 Trumpy, seventy-five feet long, white with a varnished house, a stack, a classic yacht. I love classics. Patsy was young and didn't wear many clothes. That was nice. And Bill was larger than life. He was funny, hard-drinking, a pirate kind of guy. Just what I wanted to be. I wanted to be the funniest guy in the room, the smartest guy in the room, and to the women the handsomest guy in the room. He was all those things at all times. The coolest guy in the world.

"They parked at the gas dock, the only place big enough for them. They came for two weeks. After that I didn't know where to put them. We had no slips. But they didn't want to leave."

The next morning, the Bollings were gone. Kelsey was miffed. "I thought, they never even said goodbye." He looked again. Bradley's boat was on the T-dock. Patsy and Bill had untied it and walked it to the very end of the T.

They fit *Jaru* in behind it, stern to stern. "Now two boats had the T," Kelsey says. "Patsy and Bill basically paid for Dick's slip. We became great friends. They always returned from a trip full of water, which was in short supply at Faro Banco, and needing fuel, which helped sales. They knew everyone in the boating world. *Motor Boating & Sailing* took me under its wing."

FARO BLANCO
MARINE RESORT
MARATHON in the FLORIDA KEYS

In *MB&S*, Bradley rambled on about how great Faro Blanco was. Kelsey and Eric Ball had to build more dockage on Palm Island, a 3.6-acre island connected to the mainland by a causeway. The little island formed the west side of the marina basin. "With Bradley giving us all this promotion," Jim says, "we filled up pretty quickly. We needed more slips."

Among the new arrivals were Kaptain Krunch and Raynell. They rented one of the cottages on Palm Island.

"Krunch painted all my signs for twenty-five years," Jim says. "Bolling followers, more cool people. We were so lucky to have such great people, all characters, everyone overdrinking and fun-loving, pulling pranks nonstop. We were like the Rat Pack of boating."

An unpleasant surprise was the passing of Dick Bradley in January of 1983, from cancer. In less than a year he'd helped put Faro Blanco on the map. "We parlayed being in magazines into movies and TV," Kelsey says. "We had three weekly fishing shows being filmed out of Faro Blanco. We did many movies where I supplied locations, props, extras, catering. And commercials. You want a seaplane, a sportfisherman, palm trees, dark water, turquoise water, ten people, a hundred, a beach? We got it. The lighthouse was very photogenic, and the name Faro Blanco was painted on it. The Bollings were helping us. They painted Faro Blanco as the hailing port on the transoms of all their boats. Part of their deal was to publicize Faro Blanco."

Patsy and Bill wrote a column for *The YACHT* magazine in the early 1980s. Sure enough, an article they did on dining along the Inland Waterway emphasized Faro Blanco.

Motor Boating & Sailing and other companies held their corporate get-togethers at Faro Blanco. "It was all free to them," Kelsey says. "Rooms, food, booze. It had to be."

Jaru was heavy with passengers for the spreading of Dick's ashes in the Gulf of Mexico. "There was lots of overdrinking," Patsy says. "Dick would have approved."

Jaru finally sold. It was one of those patchwork deals. The Bollings took a Mitsubishi MU-2 twin-engine airplane worth $300,000 that Patsy says was "very fancy and a bitch to land"; a two-bedroom apartment at Laver's

Tennis Resort in Delray worth $75,000; and some cash. The attorney who bought *Jaru* put $50,000 down, and agreed to monthly payments that soon faded away. "He'd listed his law firm as the owner," Patsy says, "so we had to sue the firm to get the money. It was a long process."

With no boat for the first time in many years, the Bollings arranged to rent the main house on Palm Island. Today, Private Islands Inc. gushes over this property they represent, which was sold in 2021 for $11 million:

"Situated in the heart of the Florida Keys, nested behind gates and lush tropical landscape is this grand bayfront island with a magnificent main house and two private guest houses, swimming pool, and deepwater protected dockage for multiple boats. The main two story home offers two inviting bedrooms, spacious living and dining area, a showcase kitchen and French doors that open to lovely porches overlooking the bay."

Patsy says she and Bill paid $1,000 a month for the house in 1984. As glowing a descriptive graph as Private Islands has scribed, Patsy says it is understated. "Living there, we thought we'd died and gone to heaven." She became manager of the island, caring for three houses and a pool, chores that in no way diminished the joy of living on three and a half acres of paradise with palm trees rustling overhead, coral sand scrunching underfoot, and the Gulf of Mexico lapping at the doorstep. The fact that this chronically transient couple were happy living on Palm Island says it all.

While they might have had to move ashore, their whimsy-driven life continued to get them involved with projects, like stealing a large, ungainly beacon from an airport in East Hampton, Long Island.

They were in the general area to look at an antique fire truck they thought would be perfect for Palm Island. The fire truck was indeed a joy to behold, with fresh red paint and polished bronze fittings. But it boiled over when they test-drove it. Their disappointment was short-lived. Friends (Bolling friends were everywhere by then) told them about an old airport beacon they had discovered, an item they had long thought should be confiscated and put to use.

"After a few snorts the four of us got in our friend's truck and went to have a look at this beacon," Patsy says, "which wasn't in use, by the way. We tore our clothes getting the thing on planks, but we couldn't get it into the truck." The failure to get the heavy beacon moved that night only served to increase their determination to have it. Heavier equipment was required. It became the kind of complicated project the Bollings loved, with the involvement of several other people (friends), with larger trucks and a small crane being borrowed, and with even minute progress being celebrated with quantities of hard drink. The beacon was finally trucked to Faro Blanco, where a visiting yachtsman with electronics expertise got it working.

"It had a strange voltage," Patsy says, "and it was bright as hell. It had a green-and-white prism. Kelsey eventually had it taken apart and moved, piece by piece, into the top of the Faro Blanco Marina lighthouse. It's still there, lighting up the place."

Patsy flying, not her favorite thing to do. She learned in case of emergency, and that turned out to be smart.

X

FLYING

Patsy and Bill had been living on board boats for seventeen years. Bill took advantage of the dry-land phase to learn to fly, something he'd been wanting to do. Kelsey loved the idea. He had a plane, Kaptain Krunch had a plane. Airplanes made the marina look flush. Patsy wasn't too keen on the idea. She took a crash course so she could take off and, mainly, land if necessary. It would turn out to be a smart move. Flying for her had started back in the 1960s when she was a stewardess for Bahamas Air. A British friend had a stunt plane. He'd taken her for rides and taught her the basics. "But I wasn't gung ho. You have to have so much trust in your equipment, and our equipment sat in the salt air, landed in the saltwater. No matter how much we washed it, it was deteriorating all the time, sitting at the airport in the sun."

One their first planes was a Republic Seabee, a flying boat Patsy describes as "A piece of shit. I saw fish through

Bill (right) with the Republic Seabee, and friend Bill "Doc" Munton prior to "the Wrong Brothers" first flight.

the front windshield when Bill water-looped it one time." Next was a Cessna 185 with amphibious floats. "Much better," Patsy says, "but there was always something happening when flying the seaplanes." Like approaching Nassau once when the landing gear wouldn't drop down out of the pontoons.

They were going down island with their friends Pat and JoAnn Ballinger to visit sister Rosie. With four passengers and a load of fresh vegetables, the plane was heavy, "over gross." They had to stop in Nassau to clear customs. Patsy says they were flying at nine thousand feet in gorgeous weather. About an hour out, there was a very loud, gunshot-type sound in the airplane. Bill immediately put the Cessna into a dive, a standard emergency procedure. "Bill and I had headphones on," Patsy says, "and it was still loud. I looked around. It's JoAnn's first flight with us and she's terrified. But Pat's laughing. There are potato chips everywhere. One of the bags had exploded."

With no gear, Bill had to land in the harbor. He taxied to the Chalk's Airways ramp on the Paradise Island side. Unable to taxi up the ramp, he nudged the plane against its side. Patsy jumped out and tied the plane to a rock. Bill went up the slippery ramp to talk with two customs and immigration officers, who said they had to search the plane. "But neither of them would walk through the seaweed to get to the plane," Patsy says, "so Bill carried them, one at a time, piggyback, to the pontoon. Everything was fine, groceries were okay, passports. Now we talk fuel, because we had enough gas to get to Sampson Cay, but not enough to get back. We needed twenty-five to thirty gallons more."

Chalk had no fuel, but a taxi would take Bill and Pat across the bridge to the airport for aviation gas. For containers, Chalk loaned them five five-gallon glass drinking-water bottles that were lying around. The bottles had no corks. "JoAnn and I stripped to our bathing suits and relaxed on the pontoons," Patsy says. "The guys said they could hear the bottles full of aviation fuel clinking together in the trunk of the cab. The driver asked them if they'd pay for the cab if it blew up."

Next they had to figure out how to get each of the fifty-pound bottles, slippery with fuel, to the top of the

They used their Cessna 185 with amphibious floats like a pickup.

airplane's wing, where the fuel could be poured into the tank. Using the plane's anchor line, Bill tied a barrel hitch around a bottle. Pat, atop the wing, hauled it up. Patsy held the funnel she'd borrowed from Chalk while Pat did the pouring.

"Lucky Pat was a big guy," Patsy says. "But now we were set. We cast off. I got on the pontoon and paddled her in the right direction. Bill started her up and we're ready to go. But now we are even heavier by a hundred and eighty pounds or so.

"We're taxiing in the harbor with a crazy amount of traffic, boats everywhere, confused seas from wind, current, and boat wakes. Boats are honking and yelling at us. We turn into the wind and power up, got her on the step but she wouldn't lift. She's kissing the waves. We lifted one pontoon to reduce drag, help get us off the water. We got off, but we had to fly flat for more speed before we could pull up. Here comes the Paradise Island Bridge, seventy feet off the water, sixty feet wide between columns—the 185's wingspan is thirty-six feet—and Bill says, Here we go, but we're not going to make it over the bridge, so we barely get off and fly under the bridge. JoAnn's eyes were big as an owl's."

As Kelsey says, "It was always an adventure in the Bollings' plane." Once when flying south over Greensboro, North Carolina, Bill passed out. Patsy could smell the exhaust fumes in the cockpit. She had a headache. Her window wouldn't open, so she cracked open the door and heard the engine raging. The muffler was gone. She's never been sure why she didn't pass out as well.

"I called the nearest tower," she says, "told them I wasn't sure about my landing gear, but I could see a lake and would land there." She landed, taxied toward a road she'd seen. Half an hour later a ranger showed up in an electric launch. He was angry, ready to hand out a citation. Patsy had landed on a reservoir. Drinking water. No boats allowed, let alone airplanes. Bill had revived, but he was feeling poorly. Patsy explained the problem. The ranger understood. "I suggested he drive us to a nearby airport, where we might be able to find a new muffler. First he towed us with his little outboard three miles to a beach where the plane could sit. I got a ride to the airport.

"I walk into the shop and tell the guy I've got a 185 down the road that needs a muffler. He tells me this is my lucky day. Some guy had ordered one two years ago and it was still on the shelf. I got it for half price. The next day, Bill, the ranger, and I installed it."

A nurse they knew told them to get a bottle of oxygen because it would take days to get the CO_2 out of their system. "Back then you could get a bottle from a drugstore. We sucked on it all night."

After a Speed Week reunion in Nassau triggered Patsy's return to racing, a Mini caught her eye.

XI

GONE RACING

For several years the Atlanta Sports Car Club had been working to revive Speed Week in the Bahamas. In 1984, the event was finally pulled together in Freeport, thanks to the collaboration of the Grand Bahama Island Promotion Board, the Bahamas Ministry of Tourism, and the Sportscar Vintage Racing Association. SVRA represents classic and historic cars restored to their original racing specifications. The Freeport event was meant to be more fun than serious racing. A reunion of sorts. The promoters described it as "a week-long marathon of parties occasionally interrupted by racing." More than a hundred cars were shipped to Freeport from Miami that year.

Celebrity drivers included Sir Stirling Moss, Augie Pabst, Brian Redman, and Patsy Bolling. "They gave her a car," Kelsey says, "made a big deal out of her. She invited us, so the four of us went."

The promotors loaned Patsy a Jaguar 120, a copy of the car that had burned up the first time she'd raced in Nassau. She was the only woman driver invited. "They wanted some variety," Patsy says. "I had been in several Speed Weeks in the '60s, and I was an island girl, which made it better. I was a woman who looked good in a bikini. I knew the other drivers, the real celebrities." Chief among them was Moss, one of greatest drivers of all time, who remembered Patsy from the 1960s in Nassau. And Augie Pabst, whom she had dated in those days.

Patsy enjoyed herself on the race circuit laid out on the streets of Freeport. The celebrities didn't actually race, but Patsy did get to drive a few laps in the Jag. "I didn't push it," she says. "It was a borrowed car. Although Augie came alongside in a Ferrari and we played a little." And she more than held her own at the marathon of parties. The difference was the presence of Bill, who had never seen his wife race a car. He was enthralled by the total focus that consumed Patsy when she got in a race car. He was impressed by the aggressive, professional way she drove. He was captivated by her obvious love of the game. He knew right away she should have a car and start racing again.

Patsy agreed. She's probably a sailor first, but for her, nothing quite beats the excitement of racing a car. "On a boat," she says, "you're enthused, doing what needs to be done to go fast, but you're not hyped-up. In a car, my teeth are crunched together. The adrenaline was so high I used to chew on a hunk of wood, or put orange skins between my teeth. I ended up with a mouthpiece I sometimes chewed through. In a car everything is blocked out of my mind except the instruments and other cars. I know sailing is the best, but sailing's easier, not complicated. It never riled me or scared me. Flying is my least favorite."

It wasn't until she started racing that Patsy's fear of driving in the rain was overcome. When she was nine, her father hit someone on a rainy night. "He was taking me to school in Halifax. I was in the back seat. The man he hit ended up in the front seat. From then on I was wary about driving in the rain. Racing, having good tires, provided a whole new focus."

To their credit, the Bollings never let a good idea linger. In less than a week after the Freeport event they appeared at Road Atlanta, a major track north of Atlanta, Georgia, where SVRA was running some events. The busy track would be a good place to scope out the cars. Patsy had a Porsche 356 in mind, or maybe a Jaguar, cars she had raced in Nassau. But it was a Mini Cooper that caught her eye. She'd almost forgotten she'd driven a Mini in Nassau a few times when she was just starting to race. She approached the owner, a man named Jack Woehrle, who turned out to be from Key West, almost a neighbor. He was also a fellow sailor who had owned a Hobie Cat dealership after he'd gotten out of the Navy; a sailor who had decided to race sports cars.

Woehrle had bought a Mini from a friend, then spent two years making it race ready, and (finally) convincing SVRA that a Mini was a sports car. The day Patsy and Bill arrived happened to be the day of Woehrle's first race. He had done well, beating a few Porsches and Jaguars, which also made Patsy take notice. Race ready, the little Mini had a fierce, competitive look to it, a honey badger among wolves. And it was less expensive than Porsches and Jaguars. The fact that Woehrle was just a few miles down the road from Marathon was the deciding factor. The Bollings struck a deal with him. They would find a Mini; Woehrle

Above: *Sebring (1985): Bill and Patsy (left) with her mechanic, driver Jack Woehrle and wife Lynn (right), and friends.* **Opposite page:** *Patsy leading the pack in a SVRA race at Road Atlanta.*

would tune it for them and trailer it to races. "Patsy and Bill were my first race-car customers," Woehrle says.

Bill found a 1965 Mini for sale in a performance shop in Connecticut. It was a UK car with right-hand drive they said was race prepared. Bill flew up and drove it back, an uncomfortable twenty-four-hour drive for a six-foot-two, 210-pound man in an undersized automobile. At tollbooths, from the right-hand side he had to stretch across the front seats full length to extend a dollar bill. One collector on the New Jersey Turnpike found Bill in the Mini so amusing she called him "honey" and only charged him a dime.

The same weekend Bill was en route, Patsy went to a Skip Barber Racing School three-day course being

held in West Palm Beach. "It was about rules of the road, personal driving critiques," says Patsy, who had never had any previous instruction. "We were on the track all day long, practicing race-style downshifting, threshold braking, cornering techniques, and learning to read

Following pages: Patsy (right, foreground) in the pole position behind the pace car at the start of a race in Mid-Ohio, 1985.

competition flags. The most important thing I learned at that school was never to brake when you are in a corner. Brake before the turn. In the apex of a turn if you don't have pedal to the metal you're not gaining."

"The car Bill bought was far from being race prepped," Jack Woehrle says. "Bondo had been applied over rust. I talked with Jim Kelsey. He did the bodywork, I did the engine. We had to tear the whole car apart." The first time Patsy raced it was at Moroso (now Palm Beach International Raceway) in West Palm.

What Patsy remembers about her first outing on a proper track with stands full of spectators was the yellow rookie stripe painted on the rear end of her car. She was familiar with the track, which helped. Her Skip Barber training had taken place at Moroso. "I don't remember how I finished," Patsy says, "but I didn't embarrass myself. I made a good showing. We didn't blow any engines that weekend. It wasn't pedal to the metal yet."

Racing in SVRA events meant traveling weekends as far west as Wisconsin, as far north as upper New York State. Just driving to Atlanta from Marathon took fourteen hours. Jack Woehrle, who became Patsy's crew chief, would show up wherever they were racing, with the cars tuned and ready to race. Neil Harmon, who specialized in electrics and hydraulics, had met Patsy and the team at a race in Sebring. A former steel-mill engineer from Atlanta, after he retired Harmon had volunteered at a race-prep shop in South Carolina. Today Harmon is chief of timing and scoring for the Central Florida Region of the Sports Car Club of America. In the '80s, when a team he was attached to failed to show up, he introduced himself to Patsy's team.

BY ROGER VAUGHAN • PAGE 226

"She was very competitive in a nice way," Harmon says. "You could tell by the way she drove on the track, and how elated she was when she came in, that she loved every minute of track time. She won her class regularly, finished in the top five consistently. She'd often win over cars out of her class—more powerful cars—because she could outdrive them. I've seen her dog those cars and beat them in the turns."

Patsy was doing exactly that on a small track in Saint Louis when the driver of a Porsche 356 got angry. "He had a really nice 356," Jack Woehrle recalls, "a show car. Patsy beat him in three or four races. She'd get ahead at the start and he couldn't quite catch her. It was a horrible little track, with some gravel along the edges. The Porsche guy came in mad as hell, saying, What the fuck, you're all over the road and I just got my car painted and you're kicking up rocks, and Patsy says, Oh, so sorry. I guess the way you could solve that is to get in front of me and stay there."

"As a woman," Harmon says, "she didn't expect to get favors. She knew she had to prove her talent. That's how she did it. The guys recognized her skill and talent and took her on. She fit in with the boys, no feminine role-playing, acted like one of the boys, and she was accepted. They saw how very competitive she could be. And how you could count on her to do what was required. How well she cleaned up afterward. And how much rum she could put away."

One race weekend Kelsey was walking to a party with Patsy and Bill. As they passed a tractor trailer that was parked, they heard a cat meowing. "Patsy immediately pulled her dress off," Kelsey says, "and in nothing but her underpants crawled under the tractor and convinced this kitten to come down from under the fan shroud. Saved its life." Just doing what was required.

"She always had that chunk of wood clenched in her teeth," Jack Woehrle says. "She broke a couple throttle ca-

bles because she pushed so hard on the pedal. She pushed so hard she deformed the floor in a couple cars."

"Jack beat me on occasion," Patsy says.

"She only wrecked the Mini one time as I recall,"

Woehrle says. "Racing Brian Redman. She went into a cement barrier. Not fast, maybe ten miles an hour. She was okay. Redman was good. He won Le Mans a few times."

Neil Harmon tells a story about Patsy prepping for a Vintage Race at Road Atlanta, when a young driver, a rookie, asked if she minded letting him follow her around the track to have a look at her line. She said sure, and off they went. "At Road Atlanta," Harmon says, "as a car approaches the front straightaway, it crests a hill. Then the track goes downhill significantly, followed by a right turn onto the straightaway. When you hit that peak at speed, the wheels go light. A car could take a little air. I've seen many a spin coming down that hill. And that right turn at the bottom of the hill is precarious.

"Patsy took a unique line at that segment of the track. She wouldn't brake, just let up on the throttle a little as she crested the hill, then powered through the turn to the straight. The kid following her was accustomed to gearing down. He got light on the wheels and lost it. Spun off into the dirt."

"She was as aggressive as you could get on the track," says Jim Kelsey. "Porsches, much more powerful, would pass her on the straights. Coming out of the corner she'd be first out. Biting on that chunk of wood she'd just floor it, front-wheel drive screaming, passing everyone. Then they'd pass her again. That's why she kept ruining transmissions, blowing up motors. She was tough on cars."

Patsy loved the Mini. She says other cars gave the driver a clue when they were going to spin out. "The Mini is so different with front-wheel drive, you can let the ass end hang out, so let it hang out but don't let off the gas, power through. It's completely different from a regular rear-end car. Let the back end hang out in a rear-end car and you've got to be steering in the direction your rear-end is going. In a Mini, you're turning the way you want to go. Keep your foot on the pedal and steer into it, drive out of it. The Mini handled better than a Porsche. I did lift a front wheel on occasion."

She did just fine with rear-wheel-drive cars when the opportunity arose. One weekend at the Road America track in Wisconsin, she rented a race-ready Corvette. The local drivers were all wary of a sharp right-hand turn half a mile after the start. Patsy blasted out of the start, and was surprised to see a slow congestion of cars jamming into the first turn. "Everyone was slowing down. What the fuck were they slowing down for, I wondered. Hey! We're car racing here! It was just after the start, everyone being careful at the first turn. They all went around together. I took the outside of the turn and went around them. I was third after that turn."

She liked the power of the Corvette. It was a foregone conclusion that Patsy would move on to a NASCAR-type car. SVRA had a class for the bigger, more powerful cars. The SVRA Mini class would miss her. In a chatty newsletter for the crews he was distributing at the time, Neil Harmon wrote, "What a gal. I miss her driving style—plus her no bra look at the drivers' meetings

Albert's crew, with skipper Bill Bolling (right)—Billy with life preserver—and various pets.

XII

ALBERT

In the summer of 1985, Bill had thrown his neck out. It was one of those painful, frustrating injuries making it virtually impossible to find a position that wasn't painful. He tried hanging himself from a neck brace attached to a door to try to stretch his neck past whatever was causing the problem. It didn't work. Patsy remembered a neurosurgeon from Atlanta they'd met. "Knox Kinlaw. He is a sailor," Patsy says. "He washed ashore at Palm Island one time."

Dr. Kinlaw had been bringing his Hinckley Bermuda 40 around from St. Pete to Ft. Lauderdale when he blew out his mainsail. His delivery skipper happened to be John Rumsey. "John said he knew some people in Marathon who could help," Kinlaw says. "Patsy turned on the big airport beacon at Faro Blanco, and we made it in. It was a horrible storm." Kinlaw took a shower. With a towel wrapped around him, he went to find Patsy. He thought he'd seen a rat in their shower. It turned out to be Bear, the ferret.

"It was my birthday," Kinlaw says. "Patsy and Bill fed me, threw a party. We became dear friends. I kept the boat at Kelsey's marina for several years."

When Bill's neck went out, Patsy called Kinlaw, asked if he could recommend someone to see Bill. "He said to get our asses to Atlanta and he'd fix it. Bill could recover at his house." It turned out to be a deteriorating disc requiring surgical repair. Kinlaw performed an anterior cervical discectomy and fusion, a decompression surgery, with bone taken from Bill's hip.

They never did figure out what triggered Bill's neck to go out of whack. But it could have been the vessel he and Patsy were negotiating to buy at the time. Patsy's side of the negotiation was trying to convince Bill it was a bad idea. She wasn't getting anywhere. "The more I would say no to Bill about a boat," she says, "the more his interest would pique."

This vessel was a far cry from anything they had ever been interested in. Patsy thinks Bill found it in *Boats & Harbors*, a monthly classified-ad newspaper focused on the commercial marine industry. If you are looking for an offshore supply vessel in the 180-foot range, a towboat, a sixty-ton crane with an eighty-foot boom, an industrial-sized generator, or a hyperbaric medical chamber, *Boats & Harbors* is the place to look.

Albert, a 120-foot, 180-ton patrol and rescue vessel built of steel in 1957 by the Stalsmidjan yard in Reykjavik, Iceland, was a good fit for *Boats & Harbors*.

Albert had the military profile of a mini-destroyer. Among its many other oddities, *Albert* was powered by a twenty-four-foot-long, eight-cylinder, forty-five-ton, 650-horsepower Nohab Polar diesel engine turning the prop at three hundred revolutions per minute. One cylinder was used exclusively to pressurize a compressed air tank used for starting the engine. The Nohab had direct dive, meaning there was no neutral gear. To shift into reverse, the engine had to be stopped and restarted. Warming it up for an initial startup took an oil-fired furnace two hours.

When Patsy and Bill first encountered *Albert* up the New River in Fort Lauderdale, Florida, the engine wasn't working. Nothing was working. *Albert* was a dead boat. And every gauge, nameplate, instruction sheet, and manual for every device, instrument, and system on the boat was written in Icelandic. The odd name of the vessel was the only recognizable group of letters. Turned out it was named by the wealthy man who had donated the vessel to the Icelandic Navy. He'd underwritten the total cost on the condition that they named it after his son, whose life had been saved by a similar Icelandic patrol boat.

Albert's owner was as eager to get rid of the boat as the Bollings would be three years later. In its prime, *Albert* had been a valuable player in the so-called Cod Wars, a twenty-year, unarmed conflict starting in the early 1950s between the United Kingdom and Iceland over fishing rights in Icelandic waters. Iceland had won that battle. *Albert* had been decorated. But when the Bollings first saw the vessel, those glory days were a distant memory.

"*Albert*'s ugly face," Patsy says today, recalling her first impression of the rusty hulk. "It was awful. Not as bad as *Puritan*, but the stench of mildew was powerful. Not a light worked, and it was horrifically complicated. Everything in Icelandic, an engine no one could pronounce, let

alone find parts for. Rust everywhere, everything leaked. I was not enthused. It was too big, too cumbersome, and direct drive!—are you crazy?

"I was definitely trying to hold Bill back," Patsy says. "Some of his whims, even *Puritan*, I couldn't believe he would even think about doing them. I couldn't see his vision at all. I certainly didn't see anything in *Albert*, thought it was the stupidest goddamn thing that ever came down the line. The thing didn't even have a transmission for chrissakes. But Bill loved it. He was eager for us to do one more big boat. I went along, of course. For the adventure. And I loved him. And he was going to do it anyway. The plan was to get her to Palm Island and work on her, and attract attention."

Opposite page: *A very skeptical Patsy assessing pre-restoration* **Albert.**
Above: *Bill tending the 45-ton, 650-hp Nohab Polar diesel.*

Albert was definitely Bill's fantasy, and it came cheap. Asking price was $125,000. They ended up trading their apartment at the Laver Tennis Resort in Delray for the vessel. They put Bill's son Billy on *Albert* with a small crew to get it cleaned up, reboot the electrical system, and get the engine running. It was August 1985. The goal was to get *Albert* to the Keys by Thanksgiving.

Patsy looked up the Icelandic Consulate in the United States and couldn't believe it was in Pompano Beach, ten miles up I-95 from Fort Lauderdale. She called them, said she had an Icelandic patrol boat, needed help with translation, and did they know anyone with Icelandic heritage who might have been on the vessel, an engineer or perhaps an electrician. More amazing luck. She got a call back in two days saying they'd found a gentleman who'd been the number two engineer on *Albert* fifteen years prior. He got the engine going. "The electrical system wasn't understandable even to him," Patsy says.

She called Jack Woehrle, her Mini manager (she was still racing), whose specialty was electrical systems. "They rented a Cessna 150 for me," Woehrle says. "I was a pilot at the time. Kept the plane in Key West and flew up three days a week to work on *Albert*. I fixed all kinds of things, converted electrical fittings, relabeled stuff. Between the Icelandic engineer and me, we got her going."

Bill helped. He was recovering from his complex surgery and had been told to rest easy. "That didn't mean shit to him," Patsy says. "After less than a month he was diving, cleaning the bottom and the prop when he shouldn't have been. We got the essentials going—engine, electrics, generators, toilets—so we could get her to Palm Island."

It wasn't a long trip. *Albert* cruised at ten knots while burning eleven gallons an hour, not bad for such a heavy vessel. The trip was uneventful until they arrived at Faro Blanco. The entrance to the marina is very narrow, maybe one hundred feet wide, with a seven-foot depth. *Albert's* specifications indicated it drew eight and a half feet. "We'd lightened her up, cleaned out a lot of weight," Patsy says, including hundreds of pounds of stainless nuts and bolts they'd discovered in the bilge, "and we figured if we went in at high tide as fast as we could the stern wave would lift us up and over the bump. We'd done that before. The wave runs underneath you and lifts the vessel." Not this time. *Albert* shuddered to a stop, hard aground, nearly blocking the entrance to Faro Blanco.

The usual effort to get unstuck—racing the engine full astern while being pulled by another vessel—accomplished nothing. *Albert* remained aground for four days. The Coast Guard had a station near Faro Blanco. They kept asking

Albert *aground at the entrance to* **Faro Blanco.**

when *Albert* was going to move. "At low tide she leaned over," Patsy says, "revealing years of barnacles and goo that smelled bad. People in the marina were complaining."

The full moon was imminent. "We found this guy," Patsy says, "who had a boat with two thousand horsepower in it. We made a bridle, and wrapped a thick hawser around his whole boat—not just on a cleat or two, but around the bow. On a full-moon night we had five other boats running back and forth making waves to help rock her, and when the powerful boat took a strain we cranked

Patsy smooching her ferret aboard **Albert** *during Liberty Weekend,*

up the engine. Our max was three hundred fifty rpms, and we had it hitting four hundred, and that hawser was getting skinnier and skinnier, and suddenly—wango!—

we were out like it was on a bungee cord. Did I mention the newspapers were there?"

Subsequently they took *Albert* to a yard in Key West with everyone including Woehrle commuting daily to work on her. In the spring of 1986, less than a year later, *Albert* began a trip up the East Coast, destination New York Harbor. She was looking smart with fresh paint and varnish everywhere, with flowering plants in profusion, small palm trees in pots, glass balls in netting hung here and there, and a large round table on the foredeck surrounded by lounge chairs. *Albert's* profile was still military, but the onboard ambience had a down-home, island saltiness about it that Ernest Hemingway would have liked. The event *Albert* was headed for was Liberty Weekend, being held on July 4, 1986 to celebrate the 1984 restoration (and centenary) of the Statue of Liberty. *Albert* got as far north as Jacksonville, Florida, before trouble began.

The Coast Guard cutter *Ute* appeared on the horizon at daybreak on June 4, and charged after *Albert* at full throttle. *Ute* fell alongside and got on the radio, asking for the name of the vessel, which was painted in foot-high letters on the bow, and a description. Billy was at the helm. He answered, "*Albert*, A as in alpha, L as in lima," et cetera. "We look exactly like the vessel off your starboard bow."

Billy's sarcastic rejoinder was indicative of the average boater's opinion of the Coast Guard at the time. Prior to 1975, the Coast Guard was regarded as a benevolent

Following pages: *Restored*, Albert *was impressive. But the ship's militant profile indicated some form of smuggling to the duty-obsessed USCG and they boarded the boat repeatedly.*

outfit, often coming to the aid of boaters in distress. Then in the mid-1970s came the presidential mandate for them to prioritize interdicting drug shipments, which pushed the USCG's resources, abilities, and temperament to the limit. After that mandate, reinforced with scary training films showing drug runners mowing down Coastguards-men with automatic weapons, sailors began to dread interaction with the Coast Guard. Statistics that came out in 1986 revealing that Coast Guard boardings and searches of 3,938 vessels in New England had discovered contraband on only four vessels did nothing to enhance the Coast Guard's image.

Ute went away, but the encounter puzzled the Bollings. "They had to have been looking for us," Patsy says. "They don't run full speed after every boat they see on the horizon."

With Albert at anchor in Charleston, South Carolina, a Coast Guard boarding team appeared. Albert was anchored near the Coast Guard station. They were asked to move. Bill explained that it took two or three hours to start the engine. The boarding party went away. Patsy and Bill left in the Cessna 185 to go car racing.

The next day, two US Customs agents arrived. One searched the vessel while the other man called in crew identities. They asked Billy about a hashish conviction in New York City in 1977. Billy said he'd never lived in New York, and asked what name had been checked. Customs had used an incorrect name. He suggested they try George William Bolling IV. They did, and it came back clean.

Two weeks later, while Albert was at anchor in Annapolis, Maryland, another two customs agents showed up. Patsy and Bill weren't aboard. The agents were aggressive, preventing Billy from following them around the vessel (their right). They tossed the boat, dumping the contents of drawers on bunks and going through pockets of clothing while they complained about having to work on their day off. They had improperly tied up their boat, which broke loose and banged up *Albert*'s topsides. They found nothing.

Bill had always wanted a large gun to put on *Albert*'s foredeck. He had finally found one in Alexandria, Virginia, and was determined to go get it, Coast Guard pressure be damned. Patsy was appalled. "I said, Are you fucking crazy? He said, We gotta have it!" They had started up the Potomac River to Alexandria, but had to abandon Bill's quest when they came to a bridge *Albert* couldn't fit under.

Liberty Weekend was a great success. New York Harbor felt jammed to capacity with vessels of all shapes and sizes. Aboard *Albert*, forty or more guests of Patsy and Bill's, from relatives to race-car and ocean-racing friends—including the Kinlaws, and this writer and his wife—enjoyed the extraordinary scene, the food and drinks, the animals (*Albert* was home to a large rabbit, two ferrets, and a dog), and the explosive conclusion of an unforgettable fireworks display.

Albert left New York the next day, dropped off a few remaining guests in Connecticut, and headed for Newport to continue showing the flag. A week later, while anchored in Block Island, *Albert* was boarded by the Coast Guard. "They went through the boat, again," Patsy recalls, "looked at our papers, gave us a copy of safety inspection Form 4100 so we could show it to others who might come aboard." The Coast Guard report read, in part: "The master was apprehensive at first. But brought us through all compartments. He was in a better mood when we left. No violations noted. Master mentioned previous boardings."

Albert ran without further interruption to Nova Scotia, anchoring in the LaHave River for Patsy's birthday, and returning south as far as Sag Harbor, Long Island, before it was boarded for the eighth time in four months. "Bill really got hot," Patsy says. "This one Coast Guard kid was vindictive, hard-ass. He said he wanted to do a safety inspection. We showed him Form 4100. He said it didn't matter, he could do anything he wanted. Bill called the Coast Guard. They told him the same thing. Meanwhile Billy was being hassled on the bridge." The boarding team left, promising to come back.

The Bollings went ashore to have lunch with a potential customer who was considering having a J-Class America's Cup yacht from the 1930s (*Shamrock*) delivered to Australia. It was a mad idea, but one the Bollings took seriously. When they returned to *Albert*, they found money missing from the cash they'd laid out for payroll. Having given an estimate for delivering *Shamrock* to Australia, Bolling grabbed a shower before returning ashore. In mid-shower, the Coast Guard search team returned. Bolling and crew were lined up on the stern. "Bill dropped his towel to show he was unarmed," Patsy says with a grin. Bill didn't know a woman was part of the Coast Guard team. "Now he was seen as a pervert, exposing himself." The search took the better part of an hour. *Albert* was cited for one safety item—flares—the search party could not find.

At 3:00 a.m. the next morning, *Albert*'s crew was awakened by the sound of voices. Jumping from their bed, the Bollings stepped into the glare of searchlights from several vessels. "Bill ran to the bridge in his undies and broadcast a Mayday: We're being boarded by pirates, armed thugs!" Patsy says. It turned out the "pirates" and "armed thugs" were members of the Coast Guard, US Customs, and local police.

Soon, nine men and a sniffer dog were searching the vessel, with *Albert*'s outraged crew calling them names. Accusations and denials about the missing money were exchanged at high volume.

"We almost had a problem in the engine room," Patsy says. "They wanted to pull the inspection plate on the compressed air tank. It would have left us helpless for six hours while we recharged it." After three hours, the search party departed with no violations to report.

After six boardings and two searches in the space of fourteen hours, Bill Bolling was enraged. He sat down and wrote a letter to the Coast Guard suggesting he had been robbed at gunpoint at sea (piracy!), and that the crew was so fearful "we are sleeping with our weapons, safeties off." He suggested further USCG patrols approach them in daylight, and identify themselves with a four-digit number, which he included. In closing, "lightening the tone," as Patsy put it, Bill wrote that if eight searches hadn't demonstrated that *Albert* was an orderly vessel, a full-time USCG monitor could be stationed aboard: "Of course he would have to be naked at all times, and he'd have to sleep with the ship's ferret." The letter was sent to all Coast Guard districts, US Customs, four marine publications, and two newspapers.

It was the Coast Guard's turn to be outraged. In its defense, the Coast Guard said *Albert* simply fit the profile of a suspicious vessel. In a previous life, *Albert* had apparently been anchored next to a vagrant vessel one time. The late Captain John Trainor, chief, operational law-enforcement division at the time, said such vessels had to be repeatedly checked. "The minute you leave them alone," Trainor had said, "that's when they can go bad."

A week later after dropping anchor at 4:00 a.m. in the Cape Fear River (North Carolina) after a rough, five-hundred-mile trip from Maryland, Patsy was touring the deck before retiring when she heard a small boat approaching at high speed. It circled *Albert*, went away, then came back and circled again. She alerted Bill, who went to the bridge and strapped on a pistol. The boat didn't reappear.

In the morning, *Albert* was dragging anchor. The engineer was urged to hurry the warm-up, while more anchor chain was let out. Bill, with pistol still in place, went topside to help Billy, who was cleaning bird droppings off the stack. Bill picked up the shotgun used to fire cracker shells to scare off birds. He was halfway down the ladder to the bridge when the Coast Guard appeared. He beckoned them closer to give them a copy of the letter he had written.

Patsy returned about then. She'd been ashore in the dinghy to buy a chart of the Cape Fear River. She took the letter to the Coastguardsmen, who were preparing still another boarding party. Bill had told the Coast Guard he would be getting underway within a couple hours. Communications confusion reigned mainly because of the Coast Guard's ignorance of how *Albert* worked—even

BY ROGER VAUGHAN • PAGE 246

after eight boardings. The lack of response from *Albert* to their questions and demands was taken as resisting marine authority.

The fact was that on board *Albert*, they were hastening to get going because the anchor was dragging. Bell commands from the bridge were sent to the engine room, which was a very loud place. On the bridge, the marine radio was turned way down to make voice commands from the bridge and the colorful, curse-laced responses from the engineer audible. In the engine room, the engineer and Patsy were sweating bullets as the two of them hand-lubricated the injectors and muscled the various levers and valves of the huge Nohab Polar diesel. Later, one Coast Guard officer expressed concern that *Albert* could have outrun his cutter, which actually had twice *Albert*'s speed.

It hadn't helped that Bill's anger had finally prevailed over reason, causing him to shout obscenities at the Coast Guard while armed with a pistol and waving ("brandishing") his shotgun in a scene reminiscent of Lou Kenedy's dramatic posturing when he was stealing *Sea Fox*. "It had been often suggested I married my father," Patsy says. "That was one time I had to think about it."

Consequently when *Albert* got underway and began the trip up the river toward Wilmington, there was a parade. Several "gunboats" were trailing in *Albert*'s wake. Bill suggested the Coast Guard board during the five-hour trip, but they declined.

Bill knew they were in trouble. He placed a call to a lawyer he knew in Philadelphia, who negotiated the docking scenario in Wilmington. It was a good thing, because the numerous greeters needed organizing. Awaiting *Albert* were

members of the Coast Guard and Coast Guard intelligence; the Drug Enforcement Administration; the Bureau of Alcohol, Tobacco, and Firearms; US Customs; local and state police; a US marshal; and a young assistant US attorney named

Opposite page: *Trailed by the USCG,* Albert *slowly makes its way up the Cape Fear River.* Above: *Once in Wilmington, NC, Billy Bolling was handcuffed.*

Kieran Shanahan who would later say, "We considered it a crisis—an armed vessel coming toward a populated area." The area around the docks had been blocked off. Residents and workers in the area had been told to evacuate.

Before the docking lines were secure, members of the posse were jumping aboard. It was said that Billy assaulted one seaman by sliding a deck chair into him, pinning him against the bulkhead. Billy was taken away in handcuffs, while Bill was arrested for impeding federal officers. They would be in jail four days. Patsy was ignored, one of the few times in her life she was discounted for being a woman. She immediately started working the telephone to raise money for bail and the upcoming trial. She quickly put out a flyer that read "SOS (Save Our Sailors)—a legal defense fund for a respected seagoing family who are victims of too much US Government. Please send your nickels and dimes."

Shanahan got his indictments on both Bollings for "assault, resisting, opposing, impeding, and intimidating," among other things. The charge of brandishing weapons was dropped, reducing the maximum possible sentence to three years in jail, a $5,000 fine and $250,000 in penalties.

The trial was held in New Bern, North Carolina. The results made it almost worth the $200,000 it cost the Bollings in legal fees and jobs they were unavailable to take. That number included a new nosewheel for the seaplane. When life events turn south, they seem to gather unpleasant momentum. The day of the trial, Bill, Patsy, and Billy had planned to fly in the Cessna 185 from Wilmington, where they had stayed with friends, to New Bern. Taxiing out, Bill steered into the grass to avoid another airplane, and broke off one of the nosewheels. The plane was stuck. They called their friends who were driving to the trial and got picked up. But Patsy had to oversee the Cessna repairs, and missed the first day.

No matter. Judge Terrence W. Boyle had only allocated a day and a half for the trial. He seemed to consider the case

Billy (top) and his father add signage to **Albert.**

not worthy of any more. Much to his annoyance, it lasted three days. In the end, Boyle's judgment read:

Finding and judgment - Assault on a federal officer and Aiding and Abetting. Imposition of the sentence is *hereby suspended and the defendant is placed on probation for a period of two (2) years, upon the following terms and conditions and fined the sum of $250.00.*

1. Defendant is to neither brandish weapons nor resist in any manner the boarding or search of a vessel under the direct or indirect control by the US Coast Guard or other law enforcement agency authorized to conduct same. The defendant is to pay a special assessment in the amount of $25.00.

Given the maximum penalties and fines that could have been levied, Boyle's token judgment left no question about his dismal view of the situation. In case there was any doubt, Boyle's comments from the bench about the excessive behavior of the USCG as it pertained to *Albert* was nothing short of a reprimand. The word "arrogant" was used by Judge Boyle to describe his view of the Coast Guard's application of the law.

"It was good luck we didn't get that gun for the fore-deck," Patsy says. "They'd still be in jail."

"Bill taking on the government of the United States," Jim Kelsey says, "did change the way the Coast Guard treated people, so he kind of won, but the legal fees, the nights in jail, it almost broke them."

✶✶✶✶✶✶

Patsy and Bill got a call from a charter agent in San Francisco who had seen the ads selling *Albert* in marine publications. The agent said it would be the perfect boat for taking charterers diving off Cocos Island, a tiny, uninhabited island six hundred miles southwest of Costa Rica. Robert Louis Stevenson had used Cocos as the setting for *Treasure Island.*

It sounded good to the Bollings, who saw several advantages to taking *Albert* to a new neighborhood. They quickly installed a Cascade system for recharging diving tanks, arranged to meet a qualified dive master in Puntarenas, Costa Rica, and cast off, heading for the Panama Canal.

Cocos Island was a two-day run for *Albert* from Puntarenas, but the diving there was unspoiled, and busi-

*Ironically, the Bollings happily chartered **Albert** to be used for a (failed) drug smuggling television pilot. Billy, engineer John Purdom, Bill and Patsy posed with Kalashnikovs.*

ness was good. Bill and Patsy did a few trips, then left Billy in charge and flew back to Florida. They returned to Costa Rica six months later when a buyer for *Albert* emerged. "A California guy," Patsy says. "Long Beach. He loved the boat so much he made the trip up from Costa Rica with us." Also making the trip and slipping through customs were a couple Red Lored parrots Billy had picked up along the way. "We named them Good and Evil. Evil was a biter. I put a dowel for them to sit on in a cardboard box, and we hid them in the generator."

The Bollings were asking $400,000 for *Albert*. The California buyer put down $75,000 earnest money. He threw parties on board to show off his new boat. But he was unable to get a license for the charter activity he had planned thanks to the vessel having been built in another country. He walked away. The Bollings flew back to Marathon with the down payment. But keeping Billy and crew on *Albert* was a considerable drain. A few months later another buyer showed up.

"Newport Beach this time," Patsy says. "He put down a hundred and fifty thousand and agreed to pay eight thousand a month. The money kept coming in for a couple years, then the fucker died! His father called us saying he realized his son owned us a bunch of money—around two hundred fifty thousand to be exact—and we better have a lawyer get on it because his wife was gonna tie everything up. We did. We put a lien on the boat so she couldn't sell it.

"In the end, we were in Marathon for chrissakes, doing business in California. We didn't want the boat back, so we made a deal for seventy-five thousand and an Etchells sailboat. A friend who had a truck out there that was coming back empty brought it East. We buffed up the Etchells and sold it for twelve thousand."

That was the end of *Albert*. "I wasn't for *Albert*," Patsy says, "and with the Coast Guard harassment and the other mishaps, it sounds like she was a grim chapter in our life. But Bill had his beast, and I have to say I had quite good enjoyment aboard her. Wherever we went

Albert caused a stir. We anchored up the Connecticut River off Essex when people said it was too shallow for us. Because we had friends to see. We ran aground and backed off when we wanted to leave. We anchored in front of Daddy's house in Conquerall Bank. Living aboard *Albert* was comfortable, and we had good times with a lot of friends on board."

For Sale: cougar, female, three years old, $500.

XIII

ON THE HARD

Just before they sold *Albert*, Patsy and Bill were told they had to vacate the house on Palm Island. The owners of the island, two dentists from upper New York State, had decided it was time to move to paradise. In between Vintage car races, the Bollings found a house in Marathon, close by, to rent. It had a dock allowing them to work on smaller boats, and it was next to a turtle hospital, which the Bollings found appealing. They had barely gotten moved in when two assessors came knocking on the door. The owner had decided to sell the place. Price: $140,000.

The good news was their contract on the house read that renters had first refusal to buy. The bad news: "We had no money," Patsy says. "What we had was in *Albert*. We were refused a loan by the bank because we had no assets." More good news: Eric Ball, who had sold Faro Blanco to Jim Kelsey, and who had become a friend of the Kelseys and of Patsy and Bill in the process, was on the board of the bank.

"Eric said he'd bring the paperwork to us," Patsy says, "and we'd fill it out together. He asked me how many mink coats I had. Huh? I don't have any—wait, oh yes, I forgot, one full-length mink coat. And the Buttersworth painting worth two hundred fifty thousand, and *Albert* worth eight hundred thousand, and a race car worth forty thousand . . . on and on. We've got stuff, but no money. Eric comes back a few days later and says we've got it! The bank has approved a loan for a hundred twenty-five thousand. I said, That's no good, we need a hundred forty thousand. We're fifteen thousand short. Eric shrugs and says he'll loan us the fifteen thousand.

"That was in 1986," Patsy says. "In 2023 that house was worth two point four million."

A few Sundays after the house got settled, they were lying around, which was what they always did on Sundays. Patsy was reading the newspaper when she saw the ad for a cougar, female, born in captivity, three years old, $500. A Marathon phone number was listed.

Patsy: "Jesus Christ Bill, look at this."

Bill: "Call 'em, call 'em!"

A cougar, (a.k.a. mountain lion, Florida panther, puma, red tiger, screamer) is a large wild cat. Males, at 145 to 170 pounds, outweigh females, listed at 85 to 120 pounds. Adults are six to seven feet long, including the tail. The National Park Service, reporting thirty to fifty of these cats in residence at Yellowstone in 2024, offers this advice if visitors to the park suddenly find themselves in the presence of a cougar: "carry small children . . . Do not run . . . stare in the cat's eyes and show your teeth while making noise."

"What were we thinking?" Patsy says today. "We probably weren't thinking. But we had to save this poor cougar. She was living in an awful mess. She was taken with Bill, rubbed against him through the cage."

Bringing a wildcat into your life when home is a relatively small house on less than an acre in a residential neighborhood does raise the question of what one is thinking. But as millions of pet owners know, forging a close relationship with an animal—most often a dog or a cat—can be a beautiful thing. Patsy had known that since her first dog pulled her to school on a toboggan. She'd always had lots of pets. Couple that with the siren call of adventure that drove Patsy and Bill. In addition to dogs and house cats, one could count on running into ferrets, parrots, and sometimes a large bunny roaming around in any of the Bollings' many homes. When a big cat came along—a cougar in need, as it turned out—there was no hesitation. "We thought we were bulletproof," Patsy says.

It turned out the cougar for sale had been given (as a kitten) to a woman by her husband. He had subsequently been arrested for drug dealing and sent to prison. The wife had moved to be close to her husband. A friend was taking care of the cougar.

"The caretaker was sick of the job, and was selling her," Patsy says. "Her cage was filthy with urine and poop. But she seemed calm, relaxed. We said we'd take her." They named her Christa, after Jim Kelsey's first wife.

They put the back seats down in their 1978 Buick Estate wagon and lured Christa into the way back with chicken necks. She took it in stride, lying down and munching on the treats.

When they found her, Christa had been living in a chain-link cage measuring sixteen by ten by eight feet high that included an enclosure for sleeping. The cage came with the cougar. Workmen began removing the fencing and cutting the cement-set corner posts of the cage off at ground level.

In Marathon, they put Christa in their garage, where she lived for three days while they had a concrete slab poured. The cage was rebuilt on it. They had to wait two days for the slab to dry. "Then we called all our buddies," Patsy says, "telling them to bring chairs, doors, slabs of plywood to form a movable wall that would keep Christa on track while walking around the house from the garage to the cage. We didn't know what she'd do. I had three chicken necks. She came out of the garage, all blinky-blinky—it was dark in there—and she's following me, following the chicken necks: Here, kitty-kitty. I only had to give her one. She did have a collar on, so if you wanted to, you could have grabbed her by the collar. If you wanted to . . ." Patsy laughs. "But she walked right into the cage, which was exactly the same, same water and food bowls, same bed. Same smells. All good. Then we all started drinking and praising ourselves . . . so that's how you move a cougar!"

The state fish-and-game authorities showed up. A license was required to keep a wild animal. As the game officers explained, the human keepers of wild animals required one thousand hours of training, followed by a frequent schedule of inspections. "The first time they came they told us we couldn't keep her," Patsy says. "I said, Fine, what are you gonna do, put her in your Range Rover and drive her to Palm Beach? Then what are you

gonna do with her? That slowed them down. We showed them pictures of Ozzie, the ocelot, to prove we had some experience with unusual animals. We suggested they leave Christa with us and come check every two weeks or every day if they wanted. They sensed we were decent with the cats, that we had some animal-management skills, and gave us a restricted license. They checked us in two months, then six months, then forgot about us." The Bollings contacted animal trainer Frank Weed, well known at the time for his animal show, for advice on how to feed, train, and be responsible for cougars. They bought thirty-pound frozen blocks of chicken necks from a local wholesaler.

Christa's calm demeanor turned out to be her real personality. Patsy and Bill found her behavior mostly predictable, and friendly. Bill restored several small boats while they lived at the Marathon house. Christa could often be seen stretched out in the sun on the foredeck of the boat, like any house cat, while Bill worked.

They got the second cougar a couple years later. Patsy found a nine-month-old female in Portland, Oregon, thanks to help from her niece, Tiffany Sullivan, Gabrielle's oldest daughter. Patsy and Rosie had gotten closer with both Tiffany and her younger sister, Sabrina, during Gabrielle's divorce, which had been one of those uncomfortable partings. "Mommy lived with Patsy and Bill for a while during that time," Tiffany says. "They helped build her back up. She'd visited Rosie, who helped her the same way."

An animal lover, like the rest of the family, Tiffany had a habit of scanning the pet classifieds in the local newspaper. When she saw a cougar cub being offered, for fun she sent the ad to Patsy. The timing was perfect. Patsy's birthday was coming up, and she'd been thinking about a companion for Christa. "We thought Christa might be lonely," Patsy says, shamelessly putting her own whim on the big cat.

Patsy flew out to Oregon and brought the forty-five-pound toddler home in a (large) cat carrier. "Randa," after Carmen Miranda, turned out to be a handful. It turned out she'd suffered abuse as a kitten, and was unpredictable. They kept a waist harness on her at all times. She also had a hundred-foot length of three-eighth line clipped on her. If she did get away, it gave those chasing her at least a vague chance of hauling her in.

Bill was Christa's favorite. Randa liked Patsy best. "She loved to go swimming with me," Patsy says. "We'd swim out and she'd want to come into my arms. That was my time with her. I could cuddle this cat." Patsy also liked wrestling with Randa. Both cats had been declawed, but sharp teeth left a network of scars on Patsy's arms from their grappling, some of which were deep enough to be permanent.

"You never knew when the little one was going to jump you," Patsy says. "You knew when Christa was going to be aggressive. She never bit me. But the little one didn't know when to quit. Her bites were piercing, like an ice pick, which meant there was never much blood."

My wife, Kippy, and I visited Patsy and Bill in Marathon. We had gotten to known them through *The YACHT* magazine, of which I was editor. They wrote the Full Ahead column, about the boating scene, for the magazine. Being so close to the cougars made us uneasy. Randa lived in the dining room, which had been emptied out save for a few croquet balls, her toys. We would occasionally hear one of the balls rolling stonily across the tile floor and smacking into the wall a few inches from the headboard of our bed. Randa was transferred to her outdoor cage every morning, back inside at day's end.

Bill would frequently take Christa for walks around the property. The possibility that he could have held the cat back if all 160 pounds of her had decided to go after something—or someone—was remote.

I took some photographs of her and Bill, art deco silhouettes of the cat pulling ahead slowly, of Bill angled back slightly to keep a strain on the thick leather leash—images reminiscent of outrageous high-societal

Opposite page: The Bollings at home in Marathon. Above, Patsy fillets a big fish for the cougars' dinner.

gambits of the 1930s by Londoners so inclined. Christa did not look friendly. We kept our distance. At the time we didn't know about being ready to make eye contact, make noise, and show our teeth.

Linda Mason, a reporter for the *Halifax Chronical Herald* must not have known about that either. She arrived in Marathon to write a story about the adventures of the woman from Conquerall Bank, Nova Scotia. "As I was taking pictures of Christa," Mason wrote, "the cougar was sizing up the situation, deciding her moves and the best

way to stop this invasion of her privacy. She crouched low to the ground, never taking her eyes off me for a second. She made her move and I found my right arm locked in her jaws. She retreated. It only took a few seconds. I made a quick inspection of the damage she had inflicted. I found a hole in my underarm and several bumps near my wrist where her shiny white teeth had left their mark."

Ouch. But Linda got the pictures of the big cats, and of Patsy and Bill's life in Marathon. They included shots of the short school bus that was turned into a fanciful nautical mural on wheels by the art students of Stetson University in nearby DeLand, Florida. The bus was the Bollings' escape vehicle in case a hurricane of exceptional power required evacuation. The bus had a roped-off section in the back for the cougars, and a watertight compartment on the overhead for the well-traveled Buttersworth painting. That left plenty of room for the ferrets, birds, cats and dogs, and the Bollings. It was never used for evacuation, but it logged many a mile as a party bus.

Gabrielle's other daughter, Sabrina, joined the list of those nipped by the cougars. "I have the scar to prove it," Sabrina says. "I was a kid keen to play with the big cats, and Christa bit me. She took just a little chunk. Not bad. Patsy said, We can't tell Mom, all hush-hush. A week later Mom and I were shopping. I took off my shirt in the changing room and Mother says, Jesus Christ, what happened! I said I'd knocked into a tree. She was content with that, and off we went."

Sabrina describes Patsy as her cheerleader. During her three years at boarding school in Maryland in the late 1980s, Sabrina says she'd regularly receive letters and packages from Patsy: "Letters with pictures of the cougars, the ferrets and birds, the planes, boats and race cars, Patsy in wigs and costumes. I had bragging rights. My school was a touch conservative, and my friends were in awe.

"After graduation when I decided to tour the country by myself, I couldn't tell my mom, but Patsy was my confidant. She kept track of me. She sent me one of those early mobile phones the size of a brick in case I got in trouble. She'd phone every day wanting to know my flight plan, she called it. For my twenty-second birthday she called my best friend and said, Let's get a stripper for Sabrina's birthday. My friend asked how she could find a stripper. Patsy said, Look in the yellow pages. She's our matriarch who knows everyone's birthday and keeps the logs. She has been such a rock in our family."

* * * * * *

Patsy kept racing Minis in Vintage (SVRA) and Historic Sportscar Racing (HSR) competitions throughout the 1980s. She raced at all the big tracks (Watkins Glen, Sebring, Road America, Road Atlanta, Atlanta International Raceway). She'd taken home a gold medal as winner of both Sebring and the Indy Challenge in Miami in 1985, and in 1989 won a special award during the Cooper Car Company's 30th Anniversary World Championship. She drove in more than one hundred races in the 1980s, finishing well when she didn't crash (crashes were rare), or blow an engine (several).

Perhaps her overall success in Vintage racing is best judged by the trophy she was awarded at Road Atlanta's Walter Mitty Challenge. What is currently called, simply, "the Mitty" is a weekend of racing started in 1977 at Road Atlanta by the SVRA. It's named after the well-known James Thurber short story about a character named Walter Mitty, a shy fellow whose preoccupation was imagining himself starring in all sorts of heroic, often tense situations. The Mitty, now run by HSR, is currently in its forty-seventh year. Hundreds of cars are entered by mostly "amateur" drivers, all of whom imagine themselves waving from the podium at weekend's end.

In 1988, Patsy had enjoyed a good season racing in the SVAR circuit. And she'd finished well, winning a race at the final event of the year—the Walter Mitty weekend. She was thoroughly into the post-racing partying. "I was a little oozy boo," as she puts it, and was stunned when she was called up to accept the hefty Walter Mitty Road At-

Patsy and her Walter Mitty trophy in 1988.

lanta trophy for Superior Sportsmanship and Professionalism. The applause was long and loud for the first woman ever to receive the annual award, which recognized an outstanding competitor, a committed sportswoman, and an engaging fellow driver.

A few years later Patsy had rented another Corvette for a race at Road Atlanta. She enjoyed having more power under her foot, a few hundred horsepower more than the Mini. The Corvette owner also had a Winston Cup (NASCAR) car in his garage. "MILLER" was painted on the side, and a big number 25. He encouraged Patsy to drive it. She did. "I had a good time with it," she says. "But you never know when you are losing it. You never know. It just goes whoosh! And you're gone. You go from the Mini, with one hundred horsepower, to the NASCAR car at four hundred horsepower. It's a huge jump. The Mini wheels will fit inside the rim of a NASCAR car wheel."

She liked it enough to buy the retired NASCAR Cup car Number 83, formerly driven by the veteran Lake Speed, as a historic racing vehicle. When she first drove 83, it had no power steering. Many drivers don't want it because of the extra weight involved.

"The owner said he was fine-tuning the car. It would be ready for the next race. He said I could drive it. I wasn't sure. Bill urged me on."

She sold the whole Mini package—car, spare engines, parts and trailer—for $25,000 to a man who wanted to race with his daughter.

In Number 83, Patsy raced in five or six SVRA (NASCAR-class) races over a two-year period. "She totaled the car badly twice," Jim Kelsey says. "I fixed it. It was expensive. Ten or fifteen thousand for the last one. The Mini was cheap. Number Eighty-Three was brutal."

Racing the bigger car was also taxing. "When I came out of Eighty-Three I was unable to talk for a while," Patsy says. "My jaw was locked. When I race there is nothing in my mind but driving. In the Mini I

was loose, I knew I could handle it. In Eighty-Three I was confident I could drive it and stay on the road, but I didn't always. Racing the Mini was competitive but it

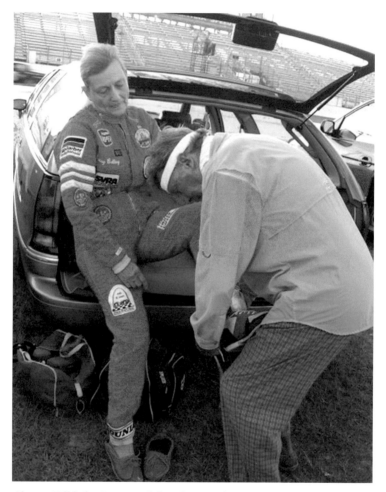

Above: *Bill helps Patsy with her driving shoes.* Opposite page: *83 after an altercation on the track.*

wasn't hostile. Drivers didn't want to damage their cars. But in the NASCAR class it was balls to the wall. They went for it. If you were in the way you got bumped."

"Gene Feldman took her out the last time," Kelsey says. "She slowed down coming into the chicane, let off the gas, and he hit her. She hit the wall, bounced off a couple times . . ."

"I'm going around eighty, braking before a corner, and Feldman tapped me. I broke loose, went up the wall, then swung around and my ass hit the wall, boogered the whole right side. They shut the track down, asked me who was president, my husband's name, what I had for breakfast."

She sold 83 for a collection of guns, a yellow dragster, and the rest in cash. She found a dealer in Newport, Rhode Island, who bought the guns, and got $12,000 for the dragster. The buyer of 83 wanted the car for show. He cleaned it up and put it in his garage under lights.

With no major boat project and no race car, the Bollings felt housebound. That was a new situation for them. Despite their demanding animal housemates and the small boats to work on, life was all too predictable. For forty years their lives had been nourished by uncertainty, by the mystery, the challenge each day would offer. Admittedly the cougars provided some of that, Randa especially, but Patsy and Bill were used to wrestling happily with more complex situations.

The word "vacation" popped up. Neither one of them could remember ever having a vacation. Everything they did involved working on a project of some sort. Even the frequent flights down island to see Rosie usually had some work-related aspect attached. Rosie's husband at the time was in marine salvage. On trips to see Rosie in Sampson Cay, Patsy and Bill would often end up landing the Cessna on the ocean and diving to examine a wreck.

That was more than okay. Work had always provided focus for what they were doing. Work was a great excuse for sailing or flying here and there. It was a fun way to keep business exciting. No complaints. The idea of turning a vacation into a project took a similar hold. Make a vague plan and go with the flow, see what happened. There was only one major problem to solve: care of the animals, including the two large wildcats.

Patsy's thirty-year lookout for potential boat projects had made her an inveterate scanner of publications of all sorts. It figured she would have come across a classified ad in the *Key West Citizen* offering the housesitting services of two veterinary students from Auburn University. She called the number listed.

"We were amazed we got several phone calls from the ad," says Dr. Michael Bailey, who had run the ad with his roommate, Jason Clark. "Patsy was one of them. She said they had ten animals. They hadn't been on vacation in years. She said, You guys come, take care of the animals. We'll leave when you get here and come back when school starts. We said, Okay, we'll do it.

"We knew they had the cougars, although we didn't know quite what we were getting into, but we figured it was a challenge, it would be fun, waterfront house and all. Neither of us had dealt with wild animals. One of them was a hundred forty pounds. The other was a hundred sixty. Massive. But we were too young to be frightened. Hobo, their dog, was the only normal animal. There were the two parrots, a cockatoo named Rags, the ferrets, and three house cats that were meaner than the cougars. We were probably more scared of the ferrets."

Jason arrived in Marathon first. Randa wasted no time welcoming him. "She bit him pretty good," Michael says. "We couldn't take him to the ER because that could have made trouble for the cougars. We nursed him back. Jason said he was never going to touch Randa again, which made her mine."

The Bollings were already on the road, having packed their Buick Estate wagon to the gills. "They couldn't see out the rearview mirror," Michael recalls.

With Randa, Michael was required to put on her harness every day, part of a lengthy protocol Patsy had written out before leaving. "She'd be growling, looking at me," he says, "but you always had that club, that stick, in your hand. We never ever hit them, or had to use it, but they saw it. If we had the club, they were fine. They'd growl, but they'd put up with what we had to do."

Toward the end of the summer, Michael had gotten comfortable being around Randa. One morning Jason was out cleaning Christa's cage. Michael casually walked into Randa's room to clean her huge litter box. Without the club. "She got me," Michael says. "In one leap she was across the room, grabbed me and slammed me against the wall. I had my hands on her neck, but I couldn't do anything with her. Her ears were pinned back. You don't realize how strong they are until they pull or push against you. Those teeth were inches from my face. I hollered. Jason came running in with his club and she backed off. I wasn't hurt. Just very scared. I thought I had gained her respect and went in without the club."

So much for forging a relationship with a cougar. One had to wonder, what if Michael had shown his teeth and made some noise? He had a good laugh over that.

All in all, cougar-sitting turned out to be a pleasant gig for Michael and Jason. Michael's father kept his skiff at the Bollings' dock and enjoyed many weekend fishing expeditions with the boys. Their friends heard about their posh waterfront location and often came calling. The parties were said to be noteworthy. Rumor was a boat had been sunk at the dock during one shindig, but it was never confirmed. Michael and Jason passed the job on to other students, who passed it on in turn for eight summers while Patsy and Bill extended their vacation project. Fifteen years later, Michael opened a veterinary clinic in New Smyrna Beach, Florida. Patsy and Bill had moved there by then. Dr. Michael Bailey became their vet.

"We loved the Bollings," Michael says today. "They were such an interesting couple, her racing with Ted Turner, and NASCAR, and him being a stuntman. And that story about *Albert*—they were proud of taking it to the Coast Guard, and how it turned out.

"Jason and I were students at Auburn, a conservative place. There was a photo of Patsy in the breakfast area without a top and a lei around her neck. Whoa! We weren't used to that kind of stuff. This was the nineties—Who is this lady?!"

******

The Bollings' vacations took on a life of their own. Nothing was ever planned. Keeping in touch with friends was where it started, and they were very good at that. Going out west would be fun. Who do we know? Call them, see what they are doing and if they'd like a visit. Talk about dates, maybe a plan will take root. Collaborate, stir it up, see what happens. And something would always happen.

They roamed around Alaska the first summer. Two summers Patsy and Bill helped her parents bring their motor sailer from Nova Scotia to Newport, Rhode Island. Several times they drove to Nova Scotia and back—a 4,500-mile round trip—stopping to see many friends along the East Coast.

In July 1992, Captain Lou Kenedy died in Lunenburg, Nova Scotia. He was eighty-two years old. He was not happy after another prolonged surgical ordeal that had, in several steps, removed both his legs to the knees. He had been spending half his time in the hospital, the other half in recovery. Diabetes was the culprit. He had prosthetics, but didn't like them. "Mommy was pushing the wheelchair, getting old and cranky," Patsy says.

"Daddy was upset. He wanted to know, Where's my leg!! It has to be with the other leg and they have to be north and south."

The end came when he choked on a sandwich. An ambulance rushed him back to the hospital. Patsy flew up from the Keys. Brian, Gabrielle, and Rosie arrived.

"Daddy was on a breathing thing," Patsy says. "Mommy says, Pull the plug. They did. We waited. Brian kept saying, Give him water, he needs water, and of course that made him linger. I wouldn't see him in the hospital. I didn't want to have that last, unpleasant memory of him in my head.

"On a Thursday night, Rosie lay up against him around ten p.m. We're all sitting outside hummin', hummin', hummin', whatever. She tells him, Daddy, the tide is going out and you should be on it, because it's Friday coming up, and you know you don't want to begin your journey on a Friday. Twenty minutes later he was gone.

"At the wake they had an open casket for chrissakes. I didn't go in. I did the gravesite thing because the casket was closed."

The Royal Canadian Legion, Branch 23, of which Lou Kenedy was a member, put on a huge gathering after the funeral service in Lunenburg. All the ladies brought food. An old salt sang sea chanties.

"Mommy was in hysterics," Patsy recalls. "We had to deal with her. I've always said that she was never one to make a whole lot of decisions, couldn't find her way out of a paper bag, but in fact she absolutely did. She pulled the plug when it was time. And for all those times he wasn't there, who was making the decisions? She was! And he wasn't often there."

Lou's headstone is inscribed: "He loved his family and tall ships."

The following summer the Bollings found themselves twenty miles north of Honduras on a very tiny island group in the Caribbean Sea called Cayos Cochinos, a biological preserve known for its marine sanctuary. Population one hundred, more or less. It was one of those "why not?" kind of trips. Joe Russell, who was working on the biography of Lou Kenedy at the time (*Schoonerman*), was going to Roatán, a larger island sixty miles north of Cayos Cochinos, to meet an old friend named Phil Richards. Richards was captain of a 140-foot motor yacht. He would take the group to Cayos Cochinos. The Bollings knew Richards because he had connected them with Gerald Gidwitz, the Helene Curtis founder who had become their financial partner in *Puritan*. When Joe suggested Patsy and Bill should join the fun in Cayos Cochinos, well, why not.

Despite the isolated splendor of little Cayos Cochinos—the largest of a group of fifteen islands, literally a speck in the Caribbean Sea—the superb diving and snorkeling, the stunning sunrises and sunsets, and the good company, Cayos Cochinos did not turn out to be much fun for Patsy. She had strolled into the woods while beach walking one day and was attacked by a horde of mosquitoes. Running frantically toward the water, barefoot, for relief, she stepped on a hunk of wood that flipped up and cut her shin. Covered with mosquitos, she hardly noticed the cut, but when she came out of the sea it was bleeding profusely. "The guys looked at it," Patsy says. "A piece of the wood was stuck in my leg. They pulled it out." They applied Benzedrine, cleaned it up, and broke out the rum.

The next day she could hardly put her foot down. Phil Richards had a charter call and had to leave. There was a little tail-wheel airplane for rent (a Cessna 170) on Cayo Borrego, a nearby islet. Five of them and their luggage were crammed into the 170, an airplane Cessna had stopped building in 1956. Specifications indicate maximum crew for the 170 is a pilot and three passengers. The landing strip was the beach. "If it was more than seven hundred feet I'd eat my shirt," Patsy says. "The whole island doesn't look that long. We're rolling down the beach and Bill's shaking his head saying, This isn't good, when the pilot says, Lean forward! to get the tail up. We take off, kissing the water, building speed so we can climb. I saw death right there in front of me. But we got up." They landed in Roatán, where there is a proper airport.

Back in Marathon the pain was bad, as were the red streaks emanating from the wound. They called a nurse they knew who paved their way into the ER at the local hospital. When the doctors got through digging the chips and residue of the rotten wood out of Patsy's leg, the one-inch wound measured four inches across. They told her she'd avoided gangrene by a whisker.

"They said I was delirious," Patsy says. "I don't remember that, but the pain was excruciating. I never gave birth to any babies, but this had to be up there. I didn't think I would die. Of all the things I've done with those fucking planes, boats, and driving, crashing has crossed my mind. But I don't ever remember thinking of myself as dead, even during that time. Maybe just losing my leg. Bill had to repack the dressing every morning. It took months to heal from the inside out. It left a serious scar."

******

It wasn't long after Patsy's leg had healed that Bill decided they needed an elephant. As Patsy had discovered with *Albert*, Bill's whims were undeniable. To this day she has no idea where the elephant craziness came from. They had ridden elephants on their visit to Thailand, but Bill had not shown interest in the animals at the time. She knew there was no way to dismiss Bill's whims. She found Riddle's Elephant and Wildlife Sanctuary in Quitman, Arkansas, a mere 1,300-mile, twenty-hour drive to the northwest. She booked them into one of Riddle's three-day training courses for potential elephant "owners," who would in fact support—financially and with visits—a pachyderm of their choice. Riddle's had no idea that a closer, personal relationship with an elephant was on the Bollings' minds.

They went to Riddle's at 6:00 a.m. every day to inter-act with their assigned elephant. "We cleaned up poop as big as a freaking couch, hosed her down, cleaned her up, fed her, tried to make her follow us. They showed us how to scrub her feet because their pads get impacted. One of the first things we were taught was how not to get stepped on. We got her into a pond and tried to scrub her with a huge brush."

After three days of elephant, Bill had had his fix. No elephant. Too much work. Not very satisfying. There was none of the usual response pet owners expect from more manageable animal companions. Or from the cougars. Even the ferrets. "Elephants are very aloof," Patsy recalls. "And they don't give a shit because they are so big. They don't care. They do what they want."

Shortly before the visit to Riddle's, Patsy had received a call from her insurance agent about their homeowners policy. The agent was following up on a rumor she'd heard about two cougars living on the property. Patsy assured her the rumor was true. The agent said that was a prob-lem. Patsy said they were just cats. Different cats, the agent said. "Don't be worried about the cougars, I told her. My husband wants to get an elephant. There was a long silence. Then she said, Please don't get an elephant. The cougars are fine."

Several summers Patsy and Bill went to Friday Harbor, Washington, to cruise the San Juan Islands on a good friend's fifty-eight-footer. The Azores were a frequent destination because Olive Adshead had moved there. Once in the Azores, why not go on to Spain? They did.

They went rafting in Ashland, Oregon. One summer they bought a van outfitted for cruising (complete with a shower), circumnavigated the USA, and picked up a stray dog along the way. On it went, summer after summer.

They loved Croatia, with its thousands of islands and gorgeous beaches. Their host was Jack Carwood, who had owned the bar in Los Angeles where Bill had met his father in the 1960s. The two men had always kept in touch.

For the millennium they were in Phuket, Thailand, cruising ten days with Charlie Thomas of Columbia Yachts, a builder that was in the forefront of fiberglass construction. The Kelseys went with Patsy and Bill on many vacations.

"The vacations!" Jim Kelsey says. "Many in foreign countries. We met so many great friends, adventuresome people, most of whom had yachts, lived on islands, loved to laugh, and drank a lot. Super-people. We were so lucky to follow along and smile and nod."

Patsy and Bill shared an undertone of irreverent humor that got them through good times and bad.

XIV

CHANGES

They had bought the Marathon house in 1986, during the *Albert* project, and even then it was evident their boat-restoration business was on the wane. *Albert* would be their last sizable boat. They restored a few powerboats in the forty-foot range at their dock in Marathon, but those were a far cry from the likes of *Jaru* and *Pez Espada*.

"We'd been restoring white elephants," Patsy says, "boats so different, Alden schooners, shrimper yachts, *Puritan*, and *Charisma*, a race boat famous for breaking masts. *Albert* was a white elephant for sure. We did well, but it changed in the early eighties. There weren't so many historic vessels around. We'd done mostly wood or steel boats—*Charisma* was the only glass boat we did—but now plastic was coming on fast. Plastic boats were a dime a dozen. You could walk down the street and find five of them in a row. We lost our niche."

At Marathon they restored a classic Bertram 31, redid the engines—bought it for $5,000, sold it for $40,000—and a forty-foot, hundred-year-old Monterey fish boat, all work they could do at their dock. The very last one was a Boston Whaler Outrage, a twenty-two-footer. They gave it all new canvas, patched and sanded it, painted it with Algrip.

In the late '90s, they decided they'd used the Keys up. It was time to move. *Where* was the big question. It took them several years to find the answer. They looked out west. They visited Pine Island off Fort Myers on Florida's west coast. They even considered buying a coconut farm. In the mid-'90s the Kelseys had sold Faro Blanco and moved to New Smyrna Beach, Florida, an attractive town on the Intracoastal Waterway a half hour south of Daytona. Patsy and Bill had rejected New Smyrna as too cold, too far north. But when they finally found a buyer for the Marathon house, they reconsidered. The fact that the Kelseys were there was a factor.

"We sold Marathon for five hundred fifty thousand after living there eighteen years," Patsy recalls. "With savings, we were millionaires for three days until we bought a log-cabin house on twelve acres of one of the last untouched Florida hammocks in New Smyrna Beach." They packed everything into a U-Haul truck and the reliable old Buick wagon for the seven-hour drive north. The cats and dogs were in the car with Patsy. Good and Evil, the cockatoo (Rags), and Christa were in the van with Bill.

Randa was absent. She'd had to live outside in her cage for three days while work was being done on the house. She had contracted pneumonia and died.

"How to move a cougar part two" commenced. Licenses were required to fence in the two and a half landscaped acres in the midst of protected hammock land where the log cabin was located. Florida fish and game commission had to inspect and approve the double fence that was required for Christa's double cage—"double" so that if the cougar's cage door happened to be left open she would still be contained.

Once again, her cage was outfitted with all things familiar. "We opened the gate, then opened the back of the van," Patsy says. "Christa stepped out, looked around. I have chicken necks. Bill's calling her. She walks over, gives him a hug, and walks in. He goes in and sits with her."

Taking it easy was not in the Bollings' repertoire. Patsy added a bunch of wild raccoons to her feeding chores. Every night she'd take a bowl of table scraps to the growing gang of raccoons that began gathering expectantly beyond the fence.

She could sense Bill's restlessness. She decided he should have a tractor for his birthday, figuring he might use it to cut trails in the ten untamed acres of woods and dense Florida brush that were part of their property. She went to Jim Kelsey for help. The tractor had to have front and back loaders. Her budget was $2,500. Kelsey laughed at that, as did those tractor owners who received Kelsey's offer. With just days left untill Bill's birthday, Kelsey found a guy with a Kubota he hadn't used in two years. The tires were flat. When they got it started and tried to lift the bucket, they were sprayed with hydraulic fluid. The owner accepted two grand for the Kubota, as is.

Jim knew a guy who said he could replace all hydraulics in two days. New tires were mounted. Jim painted the wheels, sandblasted and painted the hood. Then he sprayed the tractor with two cans of WD-40, which he wiped down. The resulting protective matte finish looked just right.

The hydraulics guy was unloading the tractor at the log house on the day of the surprise party when here came the Bollings. He quickly drove it into the woods so Bill wouldn't see it, and got it stuck. Bill was distracted while the tractor gang pulled it loose and dusted it off for presentation. They played a current Kenny Chesney song at high volume:

> *She thinks my tractor's sexy*
> *It really turns her on*
> *She's always starin' at me*
> *While I'm chuggin' along*

"Bill was all shook up," Kelsey says. "He thought it was wonderful. Then we drove it around and people threw money in the bucket. It added up to twenty-seven hundred dollars."

Bill immediately began using the tractor to build "the Nairobi Trail" through the untamed ten acres of trees and thick Florida brush adjoining their log house. "His big daily thing was working on the trail," Patsy says. "I told him to take the phone. He needed GPS because he'd get lost in there and end up going the wrong way."

"He couldn't turn his neck at that point," Kelsey says, "given the surgery, so he'd just back up until he hit something."

Like everything they did, the creation of the Walt Disney World–type "trail walk" went public among their wide network of friends. Soon, the decorative "stuff" began rolling in. A section of a railroad locomotive appeared by truck. The wreck of a small airplane subsequently labeled to have been flown by Amelia Earhart arrived, along with flight jacket and goggles. Long hours were spent hooking up scary creatures high in the trees that came swooping down on unsuspecting walkers whose passage had triggered their descent. Amusing signs were posted everywhere. Bill was understandably upset when various pieces of the decor went missing.

One summer during the trail-walk project, the Bollings stopped by our house in Maryland on one of their auto trips to Nova Scotia. Bill took pride in showing me a mean-looking rusty metal trap rated for bears he'd found in a curiosity shop in Maine. The sawtooth jaws of the big trap were fearsome. The thing had to weigh forty or fifty pounds. Bill suspected local kids were stealing items from the trail. He patted the trap: "I'll get those fucking kids."

It wasn't a joke, or an empty threat. Back in New Smyrna Beach, Bill went on the trail and set the trap, chaining it to a tree with a padlock that had a number code. While disguising it with brush, he triggered it. With a terrible CLANK! one of the teeth drove a hole through his gloved hand at the base of the thumb.

Having just locked it, despite the crippling pain he remembered the code. He managed to pick up the trap with his hand imprisoned in it and cradle it on his lap while heading for the house at top tractor speed, hollering frantically for Patsy.

Their open carport included a workshop. Handling the heavy trap with great care so it wouldn't further injure his hand, Patsy and Bill got the tangle of rusted steel onto the bench. She secured it with a big vise. With difficulty she levered the trap open and held it with big C-clamps while they eased Bill's hand off the spike. He refused to go to the hospital. "I used peroxide," Patsy says, "and Betadine, Steri-Strips, and put a rubber glove on him. It didn't infect, don't know why. But that hand never fully recovered."

In New Smyrna Beach, the Bollings had fit comfortably into the Kelseys' social scene, which was well developed. Jim was still building cars, mostly for friends or his own amusement, and he had begun creating table lamps out of old musical instruments. At least fifty people had received the unique lamps as gifts. The Kelseys added the Bollings to a regular Tuesday-night dinner get-together that has a master list of sixty couples.

Almost everyone on the Tuesday dinner list turned out to celebrate Bill's eightieth birthday. A birthday, even those of relative strangers, was a wonderful excuse for a party, and no one loved parties more than the Bollings. Parties meant costumes, lots of drinking, and always a surprise. Like the tractor. More than once Patsy had hired a stripper to entertain Bill and the guests for his birthday. For his eightieth, Patsy arranged an afternoon cruise on a friend's forty-foot sailboat on the Intracoastal Waterway. When they came in,

all the birthday guests were lined up on a two-hundred-foot dock. They all turned as one and mooned Bill. "He loved it," Patsy says, "up there on the bow in his robe, wearing a crown, holding his scepter—king of the world."

Bill's health began to fail not long after the mass mooning. "The end came slowly," Jim Kelsey says. "Not like my first wife, Christa, dropping dead at fifty-eight from a heart attack. She went from working out in the gym to dead in ten minutes. Bill just got weaker and weaker."

Thinking about all the world travels and good times he'd had with the Bollings, Kelsey went to see Bill. "We all knew he was dying," Kelsey says, "so I said to him, What do you want to do? Tell me, and we better do it as soon as possible."

Bill told Kelsey he wanted to take the train across Canada. They set off a week later. Kelsey, Patsy, and Bill flew to Vancouver. Friends picked them up. A couple days later they got on the train. "He was still mobile, but it was scary," Kelsey says. "Had a hard time walking. He refused a wheelchair, but people in train stations would see him and rush over and push a wheelchair under him . . . Sir, sit down, please. It was that bad.

"But he was still telling jokes. We took over the bar car, the last car on the train. It held sixteen people. We thinned them out until we had the right ones. If someone told a European bathroom story, everyone else had a European bathroom story. Once Bill and I were on the platform during a stop. There's Patsy in the train. She flashed her tits at us."

Patsy says Bill was in a downward spiral for two years. "He had every problem in the world," she says today, "because he'd abused and used up his body. He didn't die of cancer, heart failure, or any known entity. He just wore out. That's exactly what he did. He abused himself, well, we did, I am . . . still abusing. In May of 2013 he weighed one seventy-five, down from two hundred. In August, one forty. In October when he died, he was a hundred twenty pounds.

"He'd used it up, couldn't get more."

Bill would end up in an El Dorado (aged fifteen years) rum box, a refuge that should guarantee him a rest in peace. He was moved after his son, Billy, died of natural causes in 2023. Bill's ashes had been in an urn until then. "They wanted sixty dollars for an urn after I was paying them three thousand dollars to burn Billy up," Patsy said. "I put Billy in Bill's urn, and put Bill in the rum box."

The box has Bill's name printed on it so no one will mistake it for the real thing on Patsy's kitchen-closet shelves, where forty or more bottles stand at the ready. She's also put some of Bill's ashes in tiny ziplock bags. She always has a few of them in her purse for dispersing a dollop of ashes wherever she goes.

That included Ted Turner's seventy-fifth birthday party just a month after Bill died. Turner heard about her loss and called her up, said she'd better come to the party. "My pals took one look at me and decided they better spruce me up," Patsy says. "They took me shopping, bra, pretty undergarments, new dress, the works. The village sent me to dine with Mr. Turner."

That also included the Amelia Concours d'Elegance in 2015, when Sir Stirling Moss, OBE, was the honorary chairman. The Concours at Amelia Island, which nearly touches the Georgia border, is an important event in the car world. It is held during a long weekend in March in which a rare variety of the world's grand prix cars are on display. Moss, who was eighty-six at the time, made sure Patsy received an invitation.

When they met on the Amelia golf course, where the display of the exotic cars on the lush green landscaped carpet is totally stunning, the inductee into the Inter-

Patsy with the appropriate "urn" holding Bill's ashes.

national Motorsports Hall of Fame forgot his duties. As chairman, Moss was supposed to be autographing cars for owners and making himself available for conversations with VIPs. According to Jim Kelsey, who went with Patsy, Moss dropped everything to hang out with the girl he knew from Nassau, and whom he'd seen at the Speed Week reunion in Nassau two years before.

Slightly miffed by her husband's distraction, Mrs. Moss announced she was off to find the loo. Moss shrugged out of his blazer, gave it to Patsy to carry, and took her arm. Walking with a shooting stick, he was feel-

ing unsteady on the grass underfoot. The three of them strolled happily among the cars until they were accosted by two frantic fellows who had been combing the golf course to find Moss and bring him to those impatiently awaiting his presence.

"We thought about stealing his blazer," Patsy says. "It was covered with pins and medals, probably worth a fortune. But we gave it back."

The idea of Stirling Moss latching onto Patsy at the Amelia Island event delights Herb Fishel, who was GM's executive director of racing in the 1990s. "Back when Patsy was racing in Nassau," Fishel says, "they raced in the day and partied at night. They were fierce competitors on the track, drank champagne and enjoyed caviar together afterward. It was a loose sport. I can see Patsy walking up to Moss in the garage and starting a conversation: How you doin', Stirling?

"That wonderful lifestyle when relationships were more frequent and longer-lasting—that casual form of racing—doesn't exist anymore," Fishel says. "Today the pressure to win for sponsors, the tight regulations, the security that requires many different passes at the track, and all the inspections have taken close relationships with people out of the sport. All the awards we won for GM were great, but getting to know the people was the real takeaway for me."

Herb Fishel met Patsy in 2022 when he attended the Rolex 24, an endurance sports-car race in Daytona. It was a late decision, and the hotels for miles around were booked. Through a mutual friend, he was put in touch with Jim Kelsey, who offered him the apartment behind his house on the Intracoastal Waterway. Because Patsy lives in the house and manages Kelsey's property, she became Fishel's host. Like so many men who have met Patsy, Fishel has kept in touch. Over the last few years he's been house-hunting in New Smyrna Beach. He and Patsy often indulge their love for the hot dogs at the local Dairy Queen.

Fishel invited Patsy to the Motorsports Hall of Fame of America Induction Ceremony in Daytona. "It was a date," she says. "I had my hair done and got dressed up. Jim delivered me in his wife Susan's Porsche. It was a great time."

"What amazed me," says Fishel, who has often been recognized by *Racer* magazine as one of the most influential people in the sport, "is Patsy knew more people than I did."

＊＊＊＊＊＊

Patsy is delighted when projects come up that involve getting on the water. During her eightieth summer she heard from an environmental engineer named Bob Grady who had just traded in his houseboat on Lake Cumberland, Kentucky, for a generic forty-foot sailboat. Grady's sister was giving him grief, reminding him he didn't know how to sail, so he called Patsy, asked her to help him deliver the boat to New Smyrna. The connection was paper-thin. His sister knew Patsy, sort of. Grady had met her once through his sister. It was no matter to Patsy. A sailboat, a delivery, with teaching to boot . . . When do we leave?

"She was impressive," Grady says. "Before we left she made me get a spare anchor, a dinghy, basic stuff I now know is important. Every place we stopped she had friends. We're in the Noose River, it's blowing twenty, she says, Let's see what this boat can do. I'm hanging from the superstructure. She's on the leeward side, hand playing in the water. I'm asking if we are safe.

"She taught me everything. In her straightforward way she's asking me why I'm doing this or that. She's coaching, Slow the boat down, Bob, coming to bridges. Her vigor and enthusiasm is catching. Somewhere during that trip I fell in love with her. That's the only way to say it."

Her next invitation would be grander.

Puritan *racing in a classic regatta at Cannes.*

XV

GUEST ON BOARD

During his initial phone call responding to Patsy's offer to help him understand the yacht she'd helped restore in the 1970s, Tomas de Vargas Machuca, *Puritan*'s new owner, had said she should come sailing sometime. That's such an easy thing for a boat owner to say. It's just as easy for a busy boat owner to forget about it. Not Tomas de Vargas Machuca.

His family descends from Nicolás Tomás Luna de Vargas, who accompanied King Alfonso VI of Castile in the conquest of Madrid in 1083. He established his stately home there. It's one of the oldest estates in Spain.

In his early forties when he bought *Puritan*, Tomas was co-CEO and chairman of the executive committee of Adler Real Estate, a German-based company specializing in affordable housing. Previously he'd been a vice president of Credit Suisse, and executive director of UBS Investment Bank. Tomas's mother is American. His late father, a refugee from nobility and owner of a television advertising agency, instilled a working sensibility in his son.

Since his early years, automobiles have been Tomas's primary passion—another legacy of his father's. He is currently chairman of HERO-ERA (Historic Endurance Racing Organization—Endurance Racing Association), the premiere organization for international rallies of classic automobiles. The 9,317-mile Peking to Paris Motor Challenge is one of HERO-ERA's major events.

Tomas came to sailing later in life, but with no less enthusiasm, and with the same emphasis on the classics. Before he bought *Puritan*, he had restored *Orianda*, an eighty-foot schooner also designed by John Alden (1937). Tomas collects 10-meter yachts built in the 1910s and '20s. He owns five of them.

Tomas's follow-up call to Patsy came a year later. In the interim, *Puritan* had undergone a big refit. Tomas had had the hull restored along with the centerboard, the heads, the main engine, and air-conditioning. He'd installed new topmasts, built a new galley, replaced turnbuckles, improved the hatches. "Just replacing the prop and shaft is a crazy job," Patsy says. "The shaft is forty feet long. It's offset. It leaves the engine and goes off on a slant and exits the port stern by the rudder. There are three aligners [pillar blocks] along the way." There wasn't any rebuilding. They just made everything work. *Puri-*

tan was back in a Lloyd's Register A-1 rating. "He said I should come to Saint-Tropez," Patsy says. "I couldn't go at the time. Meanwhile we had conversations about various aspects of the yacht."

Tomas called again a few months later. Monaco Race Week was coming up, and he was intent on getting as many previous owners of the yacht as possible on board.

Vernon Gray (left), Patsy, and Tomas de Vargas Machuca.

He invited Vernon Gray, grandson of the original owner. He invited the children of Oskar Schmidt, the man who had bought *Puritan* from the Bollings. He invited Patsy, and Olive Adshead.

"I invited Patsy," Tomas says, "when I heard the tone of her voice on the phone, her friendliness, and her saying she had plenty of books, and she could tell me what they did to the boat. At the same time we got hold of Vernon Gray, whose grandfather had commissioned *Puritan*—

that was a great circle—and they both happened to be close to where my mom and stepfather live in Vero Beach. Vernon and Patsy, a no-brainer. Then when we met in person—if she was so fascinating on the phone, you can imagine what the real-life Patsy experience is all about.

"She reminds me of this amazing Italian lady Iria Bonzi, who is about the same age as Patsy. Bonzi was a very capable hunter who traveled the world. She did many pioneering activities, like skydiving and hot-air-balloon travels. Patsy is significantly prolific in her motoring adventures, her very adventurous life. She is one of those rare women who are as resilient as any man, but who do not lose their femininity. She needs no pampering. She's on it: graceful, elegant, fascinating for all the things she has done."

"I was a little nervous about going alone," Patsy says. "A treat would be Olive. It was a stretch. I had to pay for me and Olive. In Monaco I rented a car, but parking was impossible. We stayed out of town, took the bus in every day.

"The first evening we walked down the quay in front of the Monaco Yacht Club, and just looking at the masts both Olive and I could tell *Puritan* from afar. We were dressed in our best with big canvas bags full of photos and scrapbooks. We were greeted by Simon Pandolfi, *Puritan*'s captain. And Tomas.

"Tomas! I couldn't have imagined a better-looking, more gracious young man who also had enough money to afford this vessel and, with his consortium, put her in such gorgeous shape. He is so easy to get along with, so hospitable, so generous, wanting to know every detail about the schooner, why was this here, why was that there

... If I had been thirty years younger I would have run off with him."

Cocktails began at seven. Dinner was at ten. "We talked and showed pictures," Patsy says, "passed books around. Tomas was totally into it, looking at all the photographs, asking questions.

"The yacht is absolutely breathtaking. Gold faucets! And the engine room is now packed with water makers and ACs. We had AC, but ours was cold water pumped through pipes. Antique, but it worked. Now it's got Wi-Fi, everything that's needed in this new world. The rebuilt engine gives her more speed, and it's a bit noisy, but you're not gonna use this boat as a getaway after you rob a bank."

They sailed four days in Monaco Race Week. *Puritan* needs a crew of eighteen people for racing. Hoisting all seven sails with a green crew takes nearly an hour, half that by season's end. There are two winches for the jib, and two winches for the jib tops'l. Everything else is done by hand. It takes eight to ten people lined up on a sheet to raise or trim a sail like it's a tug-o'-war. *Puritan*'s priority isn't winning. It's showing everyone it's possible to sail a big yacht in a traditional manner.

"I was laid-back," Patsy says. "A guest aboard. But I know the best place to be for seeing everything is aft of the wheel, where the afterguard hangs out. I made a spot for myself there with the boys in the back. Scottish fellows. I knew they'd talk. I told them I could help, tail lines, whatever, do the backstays. I could help! I'm not sure how it went off, but they accepted me immediately. I was in. Although I didn't get to steer for a couple days."

Puritan has two captains. Simon Pandolfi is the professional in charge of the boat. Captain David Martirano comes aboard for racing.

"I saw Patsy was immediately working with the crew," Martirano says, "not sitting around being a VIP guest. She was helping get the boat set up. When I walked on board she introduced herself to me right away. I'm a Nova Scotia guy. I recognized her seafaring accent. She knew I ran *Eleonora* for four years, a legendary 160-foot Herreshoff schooner launched as *Westward* in 1910. We hit it off right away."

"I would say to the boys, hey, grab that backstay because it's starting to fly, or something," Patsy says. "They hadn't seen it. But I see things, like how slowly the boat would tack because they were just turning the wheel hard over, and I thought, Holy fuck, they aren't even backing the forestays'l to help it! But I just had to suck it in and then carefully bring

Below: Puritan racing at Cannes Regates 2018, *painting by Shane Couch.* **Following pages:** *A spread of* **Puritan's** *elegance; and* **Puritan's** *Captain Simon Pandolfi with Patsy at the helm.*

it up in the evening over a rum, like, Why do you do it this way? I didn't want to be too pushy, which I can be."

Simon Pandolfi has to laugh when he recalls Tomas telling him there would be an old lady coming aboard. "As you can imagine, I expected everything but what Patsy is," Simon says. "She's a force of nature. When Tomas told me she'd saved the boat, I didn't understand he literally meant she'd done it with her hands—how she and her husband were the hearts, the minds, the brains behind the restoration."

"Within a couple days, I'm steering," Patsy says.

"You can imagine my anxiety when this lady says would I mind if she takes the helm for a while," Captain Simon Pandolfi says. "I say of course, but I keep an eye on her, pretend I am looking somewhere else, but my full attention is on her, and after a few minutes I realize there is no need to pay attention to her. She was like already part of the crew. She could steer *Puritan* like it was the last thing she did yesterday. Like she never left. At the same time she'd be more than happy to go to the runners if there was lack of a deckhand. The spirit of crewing that she has never forgotten made her so welcomed and loved by our young crew. Incredible, isn't it? She'd be hoisting sails if I'd let her. It's like she's in her fifties. Her brain is as elastic as a young person's. I think her secret is to drink a bit of rum every day."

"She knows the boat like the back of her hand," says Martirano, who gave Patsy time at the helm while racing. "She told me how we should be steering the boat, that we were trying to steer it too sharply instead of letting her bear off a bit for speed, then easing her back up, and tacking more slowly instead of slamming the boat over. How one quick tack with the rudder hard over stops the boat. Ease the main a bit in the tacks and let her get speed up before you trim. She's coaching me, and I appreciated it because I hadn't driven this boat before. Its mechanical steering was different from what I was used to.

"She had a little smirk on her face, a sharp glint in her eye, when she took the helm and the boat started moving a knot faster. She has a good eye to weather, sees the puffs, lets the boat ease up into them. Her tacks are nice and slow to maintain momentum. She looked at me and winked. I just smiled back at her. Not everyone knows how to sail a gaff-rigged schooner. For Patsy it's like dancing with an old boyfriend."

Patsy quickly became "Auntie Patsy" among the crew. The boys posted this on Tomas's Classic Yacht Experience website (for his Puritan Foundation) after Patsy's visit:

She hops on board with the poise of a debutant and immediately charms everyone around her with a perfect combination of witty anecdotes and stories about the many yachts she's helped restore over the years. "You want to know why there's a patch on the gunwale back there," she asks? "It was New Year's eve 1973. As midnight struck I was the one tasked with firing the saluting cannon. In retrospect, I might not have been the most qualified person to aim the damn thing."

She diplomatically omitted the fact that alcohol had been involved.

"We run a sort of volunteers academy where we try to train young boys," Simon Pandolfi says. "Every one of them who meets Patsy falls in love with her. They stay in touch with her, ask her advice, share their moments with her as part of the crew. She's always been able to deal and connect with owners, guests, and crew in the same way, with the same easy manners, with the same civilized approach. And with amazing humbleness that comes out of nowhere considering the experience she has. It's a great pleasure to sail with her."

It turned out Tomas spends Christmas every year with his mother and stepfather in Vero Beach, Florida. Patsy always has Christmas with Rosie in nearby Jupiter. During Christmas week, Tomas invited her to join his family for lunch at their club. They had such a good time she was invited back for New Year's. Patsy arrived with a mince pie and poppers for everyone, a European tradition. They spoke about Tomas's family's annual summer trip to New Hampshire and the difficulty of finding a sitter for their two cats. Patsy said look no further. She has frequently housesat with mother's cats. When she and her husband planned a four-month trip to Europe, Patsy collected the cats and brought them to New Smyrna Beach.

She's been invited back to *Puritan* many times. "The time I most enjoyed," Patsy says, "was when we were sailing from Monaco to pick up some royals who were coming aboard. We were motor-sailing with everything up, doing nine to ten knots, just lovely. I was at the helm and I had the whole fucking boat to myself. Not a crew on deck, not a person around. Just me and *Puritan* stretching out in front of me, and I thought, Here I am. Wished I had a drone to get a picture. A crewman came up and said he'd be happy to take over. I told him I'm only going for a pee and I'll be back—I'll be right back."

When Patsy turned eighty in August of 2023, Tomas invited her for a four-day cruise. The boat was hers for four days. Happy birthday. "Without her intervention," Tomas says, "we would have lost *Puritan*. If you have her dynamic approach you can be almost eternal. Patsy is timeless. She's this mystical character. She's a very good room reader. She'll know exactly what conversations to have with people.

"She's been inspirational with everything we've done on *Puritan*. She's old-school, an encyclopedia of how sailing and yachting was done when it was much tougher than today. We're trying to keep that authenticity alive, and she knows how to do it."

At this writing, Tomas is weighing his options for keeping *Puritan* alive. Selling her is a possibility. More likely is maintaining the Foundation under which *Puritan*'s authenticity can be insured. "Whatever form it takes," Tomas says with a chuckle, "we intend to lock Patsy away in the engine room so she'll go with the boat."

Patsy (red hat) navigates for Tomas de Vargas Machuca in the 2024 Flying Scotsman Rally

XVI

CLASSICS

Knowing that Patsy's love of race cars had four wheels and a finely tuned engine in common with the rallies he runs as chairman of HERO-ERA, it was only a matter of time before Tomas de Vargas Machuca would lure Patsy into one of his classic cars for an adventuresome cross-country rally. The country was northern Scotland, bloody cold in April. The event, the Flying Scotsman, is a six-hundred-mile rally over three days on narrow country roads from Chester to Auchterarder. Tomas would be driving. Patsy would be his navigator. She was told to dress warmly, in period clothes please, and oh yes, don't forget to bring something dressy, also period, for the awards dinner at the elegant Gleneagles Hotel in

Auchterarder, which opened its doors in 1924.

It was an irresistible invitation. Tickets arrived. Patsy began packing. The fact that it was the rainy season, with temperatures ranging from twenty-eight to forty-one degrees Fahrenheit, was never a consideration. As Tomas said afterward, "Ah yes, April in the north of Europe—it's where tough people go to enjoy themselves."

A car rally is described as "an automobile competition over a specified public route with a driver and navigator attempting to keep to a predetermined schedule between checkpoints." "Attempting" is the key word here. While always a challenge, the intricate rules and procedures of a rally are routine to frequent players. For a novice like Patsy, the heavy book of maps, diagrams (called "tulips"), and instructions the navigator is meant to quickly digest and communicate to the driver—turn left over the next rise; slow down, bad corner ahead; gas station in 6.3 miles—who is busy drifting through a dirt-road corner at sixty miles an hour, is daunting. "The book may as well have been written in Chinese," Patsy says. "Or Greek. It was nuts. Nothing made sense. And there was no fuel gauge in the car. It held forty-five liters (twelve gallons). At seventy miles per hour, we had to fill up every two and a half hours." Roughly fourteen miles per gallon.

The (open) car Tomas chose for the event was a 1926 3/4.5-liter W. O. Bentley, bodied by Henley Coachbuilders, London. All the entries had to have been built prior to 1935. The list of the sixty-one cars entered read like a fantasy world of exotic antique automobiles. There were several models of Bentleys, Aston Martins, Rileys, and Jaguars. There was also a Lea-Francis Hyper, a Talbot

AV105, a Frazer Nash-BMW 328, and several others only an automobile historian would recognize. And there was a 1929 Rolls-Royce estate wagon with wood trim that had belonged to Stirling Moss's father. He'd used it to tow a trailer bearing his son's race cars.

"It was out-of-this-world unbelievable," Patsy says. "What amazed me the most was here were all these half-million-dollar antique cars, give or take, coming to the start all shiny and bright, like a concourse d'elegance. Then the first day you go through the deep water puddles, and you're squealing and sliding into the mudbanks, then you run through pig shit or cow shit and smell like it till the rain washes it off. You're doing this often at seventy miles an hour. It gets muddier and trashier and smellier. How they can take those amazing cars and trash them I don't know."

One day they encountered the Moss Rolls-Royce broken down. Turned out the car was overheating. Patsy

watched as the navigator pulled a bucket out of the back, ran down to a stream and filled it, poured it into the radiator, and off they went.

At day's end, the competitors gather at the appointed hotel, put tonneau covers on their cars, have a few drinks, shower, enjoy an excellent dinner, and go to bed around 1:00 a.m. or whenever the bar closes. "You get up at six," Patsy says, "have breakfast at seven, leave at eight thirty in your mud-trashed car, and try to find your way to the next stop."

"The navigator's job is difficult," Tomas says. "One has to calculate time, interpret maps, figure out difficulties, negotiate with the driver while the elements batter you. This was not a walk in the park. It's tough, like getting some club sailor on a boat and asking them to be tactician in a pretty important race."

As chairman of HERO-ERA, Tomas has access to the best navigators on the continent. One had to wonder why he would invite a novice like Patsy to ride shotgun with him.

"For someone who's had the extraordinary life she's had, the fact she's so resilient, so appreciative of her adventures," Tomas said, "made her a perfect candidate. I wanted to share the rallying with her. We'd talked so much about it on *Puritan*. Putting her in the car was the only way to do it. She's not someone you invite to watch things. She has to be if not in the driver's seat, then in the navigator's seat."

They got second in their class, but Patsy wasn't happy with her work. "Tomas was a fantastic teacher," she says, "but being used to driving on the right side of the road, I had a mental block going around those cones that were part of the course. Couldn't get it right."

"The first day was a bit discombobulated," Tomas says. "You can't explain the job, you have to be in the car and figure it out. Patsy's competitive. She wanted to excel, make it perfect. For me it was perfect, whatever the outcome. It was a pleasure to be with her in the car."

"Tomas is so comfortably diplomatic," Patsy says. "Everything to him is beautiful, special, or rare. Nothing much bothers him."

Opposite page: *The Bentley's finish at Gleneagles Hotel. Tomas and Patsy won second place in their class.*

Patsy was singled out by the master of ceremonies at the gala dinner at Gleneagles. Having done his homework, the MC related tales of her early racing days in the Bahamas; her many successful years in the Mini and her high-tension NASCAR events; her ocean racing with *American Eagle*; how she'd had to sell her Bentley to help purchase *Puritan*; and how it had come full circle, as she was back on *Puritan* and now Tomas had given her a ride in his Bentley.

"I had to go onstage, say a few words," Patsy says. Her fancy period dress was a long skirt, a knee-length equestrian jacket over a white blouse, a small brown hat bearing auto pins and gears clipped on, and gold sneakers. "I'm old enough now that I don't have to explain myself or wear high heels to do anything," she says. "I told them I could get around the buoys on a boat, but had a hard time in a car." She presented the sportsmanship award. Later she suggested to Tomas that HERO-ERA create a hard-luck trophy like the one she received in Nassau when her first car caught fire, an idea he liked. (When his 1914 American LaFrance car caught fire during the 2024 thirty-seven-day Peking to Paris rally, Patsy would have her 1961 trophy reengraved and sent to Tomas as the second Hard Luck recipient. If she can find it.)

The next day Patsy and Tomas drove south four hundred miles to his country estate in Bicester, ninety minutes north of London, where he has an office. He is also a shareholder with the Bicester Heritage, the UK's only hub for historic motoring appreciation. It is an impressive automobile complex involving fifty specialized, car-related businesses.

Classic cars are everywhere on the large Heritage campus. It's also headquarters for HERO-ERA. There was to be a royal visit to the Heritage from Prince Michael of Kent, who was on tour with the prince of Kazakhstan. Since the prince is a young man interested in cars, the Bicester Heritage was a must-see. But it was another nasty day. Rain and high winds closed airports along the route.

"It was ridiculous," Patsy says. "Tomas was driving with no hat, wearing gloves with the fingers cut off, at seventy miles an hour in freezing conditions. I've got my elbow over the edge of the door to keep from slipping on the seat. Before we left he said we could put the hood [top] up if I wanted. I said, What do you think? He said, We never drive the car with the hood up. The sun came out as we approached the barn in Bicester."

"It's the stuff of heroes, really," Tomas said.

******

Back in New Smyrna Beach after fourteen hours of traveling, Patsy had less than a day to unpack, repack for hot weather, have a quick bike ride, and make a plane to Antigua for more classic racing. This time it was a four-day event on a somewhat friendlier vessel, an Alden schooner built in 1929 that had been restored by Alex Child, a former *Puritan* mate she'd gotten to know. The event was the Antigua Classic Yacht Regatta. Days started at 6:00 a.m. making sandwiches with two loaves of bread, putting aboard cases of water and beer, and leaving the dock at 9:30 for a 10:30 start.

"It was worth it," she said upon her return, "but I abused my body beyond recognition, trying to do things that thirty- and fifty-year-olds were doing. I'm fucking eighty! I trashed myself. It's okay. I'm in decent shape, but one hand was for me, totally, the other for the boat. I'm moving all the time, trying to find my way to the foredeck, or get out of harm's way, on the cabin top, tacking now, hoping the boom doesn't get me, stretching, sliding down the deck . . . My ass is fucking raw from shifting around on the teak deck without a cushion. Like when you ride long distance on a bicycle. Absolutely raw. After racing we'd come in and get free rum that tasted like kerosene, drink and tell stories until 1:00 a.m. Total abuse."

Sisters (from left) Gabrielle, Rosie, and Patsy in 2003.

A week later Patsy went to Harbour Island off the north end of Eleuthera, sixty or so miles northeast of Nassau, for the wedding of her niece Sabrina. She drove to pick up Rosie in Jupiter, and they flew out together. With Gabrielle in her fourth year of memory care, Patsy was asked to be mother of the bride. "I had to make a speech," she said. "No idea what I said because I was quite inebriated, but everyone said it was okay." With the rehearsal dinner, the wedding, and two birthdays among the family members present, not to mention the great diving and riding horses on Harbour Island's famous pink beaches, it was a busy week.

Patsy and Rosie with their niece Sabrina at Harbour Island.

Back home, Patsy was getting into her old routine, pausing phone conversations to exclaim about noteworthy boats passing by her window on the Intracoastal Waterway. She was caring for Tomas's mother's cats for a month, which was slightly altering the household dynamic. It seemed that Cooper, Billy's dog she'd inherited, liked cats, but the cats' jury was out on Cooper.

"I had my usual ride on the beach this morning," she said. "It was gorgeous. Tomorrow I'll be back on the rowing machine."

The week she returned there was a good turnout for the Tuesday dinner. Then on Saturday night Patsy and a bunch of friends went to Casey's Bar, a New Smyrna Beach favorite. "This handsome guy asked me to dance," Patsy says. "Oh my God he was so good-looking, leaning me back on his arm. We had a ball. His wife came up to me and said, I'm so happy you can dance because I don't dance very well . . . he finally has a good partner. And I said to her, Thank God that you came up, because I really wanted to hit on him, he was so good-looking.

"It was such fun. If you can do it, do it, and I'm doin' it."

Patsy with the author and his cat, Wanda.

Merry Christmas
2002

SURF'S UP!·

WANTED

BY THE F.B.I.
$50,000 REWARD

REPENT

Peace on Earth
1998

from BONNIE & CLYDE

Peace
Moral Compass
Adjusters

Fr. Balducci &
Sr. Patricia

**Best of Luck
in Your Golden Years
From Dawson Charlie & Klondike Kate**

*Happy
Holidays*

Plug Into Holiday Fun.
Hugs & Sparks.
Patsy & Bill

Merry Christmas & Happy New Year

2015

PATSY'S RUM TASTING NOTES

Brand	Origin	Age	Comment	Date
1 Barrel	Belize	?	A bit of a bite	2/17/2020
896-5	Barbados	5	Nice, Smooth sipping	5/26/2021
896-8	Barbados	8	Smoother, tasty	5/26/2021
Abuelo Anejo	Panama	5	A good one	4/19/2023
Afrohead	Trinidad	7	OK	3/29/2021
Angostura 5	Trinidad	5	Nice	8/4/2021
Angostura 7	Trinidad	7	Good	8/9/2015
Appleton 8	Jamaica	8	Balanced, stable	8/4/2021
Appleton 12	Jamaica	12	Bit of bite, better on ice.	10/25/2023
Appleton Estates	Jamaica	?	*no entry*	5/5/2014
Appleton Signature	Jamaica	?	Mellow	3/29/2021
Atlantico Reserva	Dom. Rep.	?	Sweet & Rich	1/25/2021
Atlantico XO	Dom. Rep.	?	Needs ice/Sweet	12/30/2018
Baccoo 5	Dom. Rep.	5	Sweet, better with ice & soda	4/10/2022
Baccoo 8	Dom. Rep.	8	Sharp, middle of the pack	2/17/2020
Baccoo 12	Dom. Rep.	12	Rich caramel, better on ice	5/19/2022
Barbancourt 4	Haiti	4	Good	5/26/2021
Barbancourt 8	Haiti	8	Slightly strong but good	3/29/2021
Barcardi 8	Puerto Rico	8	Tasty, Very good	9/26/2019
Bacardi 10	Puerto Rico	10	Very good	4/19/2023
Bacardi Anejo Cuatro	Puerto Rico	4	Smooth, mild vanilla	5/18/2022
Bacardi Gran Res. Diez	Puerto Rico	10	Good Solid Rum	5/19/2022
Bacardi Res. Ocho (Rye)	Puerto Rico	8	Mellow, nice flavor	10/25/2023
Bacardi Res. Ocho (Org)	Puerto Rico	8	Slight Bite, Rich	10/25/2023
Barcelo Imperial Onyx	Dom. Rep.	?	Very Good	4/19/2023
Barnacles	Dom. Rep.	8	Heavy Vanilla, sweet - best with ice	5/19/2022
Blackwell	Jamaica	?	Molasses flavor	8/9/2015
Blackwell Black Strap	Jamaica	?	Heavy Molasses, Strong	*no entry*

Brand	Origin	Age	Comment	Date
Bayou Rum Reserve	Lacassine LA	?	Smooth, well balanced	1/3/2022
Bohemio	Panama	15	Strong & rough	3/29/2021
Botran	Guatemala	12	OK	*no entry*
Bounty Premium Gold	St. Lucia	?	Light & Subtle	5/19/2022
Brugal 1888	Dom. Rep.	?	Oaky, not as good as Anjeo	5/26/2021
Brugal Anejo	Dom. Rep.	?	OK, smooth	8/9/2015
Brugal Anejo Superior	Dom. Rep.	?	Very Good	10/25/2023
Brugal Extra Viejo	Dom. Rep.	?	Smooth, Very Good	5/19/2022
Bully Boy	Boston	?	Carmel/Medium Body	6/19/2024
Bumbu Spice	Barbados	?	Strictly for Hot Toddys	*no entry*
Calazan	Venezuela	2	smooth, good	8/4/2021
Calazan Ron Anejo Prem.	Venezuela	6	Rich but balanced, leans to sweet	1/25/2021
Calazan Ron Anejo Spec.	Venezuela	2	Rich but balanced	9/3/2020
Canasteros	Colombia	8	Smooth, nice	2/17/2020
Canasteros	Colombia	15	Very good	11/29/2021
Cane Royale Gold Rum	*no entry*	?	*no entry*	5/8/2016
Captain Bucanero	Dom. Rep.	?	Sweet, heavy vanilla	*no entry*
Carupano Reserva 12 Excl.	Venezuela	12	Smooth in '21, not so in '24	3/29/2021
Carupano Reserva 6 Esp.	Venezuela	6	Rich, but balanced	1/25/2021
Cayman Reef	Barbados	5	Mellow	1/25/2021
Centenario 9	Costa Rica	9	Smooth and Tasty	8/4/2021
Chairman's Reserve	St. Lucia	?	Smooth and fruity	8/4/2021
Clement	Martinque FWI	?	Heavy Vanilla, no Rum Taste	10/25/2023
Cruzan (Amber)	St. Croix	?	Quite good	8/9/2015
Cruzan 151	St. Croix	?	Too much, punch rum only	*no entry*
Cruzan Aged Dark	St. Croix 2	?	Very Good, Balanced	1/25/2021
Cruzan Black Strap	St. Croix	?	Heavy Molasses, Strong	12/30/2018
Cruzan Single Barrel	St. Croix	?	*no entry*	5/8/2016
Cruzan S. B. Extra Aged	St. Croix	5-12	Good Solid Rum, A bit tough, oaky	8/9/2015
Dictador Amber 100	Colombia	8.3	Balanced	9/26/2019
Diplomatico Anejo	Venezuela	8	Top quality	2/17/2020
Diplomatico Matuano	Venezuela	8	Smooth, very good	1/19/2016
Diplomatico Res. Excl.	Venezuela	12	Soft, gentle	2/15/2021
Doc Brown	New Smyna B. FL	?	Alcoholic syrup	3/29/2021
Don Moderas Multi	*no entry*	5+3	Very Good, smooth	2/17/2020
Don Pancho Origines	Panama	8	A bit sweet, better on ice	11/29/2021
Don Papa	Phillipnes	7	Sweet & Rich	1/25/2021
Don Q Anejo	Puerto Rico	3	*no entry*	12/30/2018
Doorly's 12	Barbados	12	A bit sharp, better on ice	5/26/2021
Doorly's 8	Barbados	8	Very Nice	8/9/2015
Doorly's XO	Barbados	?	Good Rum	1/19/2016
Dos Maderas	Spain	5+3	Very smoooth	2/17/2020
El Dorado 5	Guyana	5	Good	4/10/2022
El Dorodo 8	Guyana	8	Good	4/30/2015
El Dorado 12	Guyana	12	Good one	5/8/2016
El Dorado 15	Guyana	15	A little sharp. 12 is better	2/17/2020
Flor de Cana 18	Nicaragua	18	Very smooth	3/29/2021
Flor de Cana Anejo Oro	Nicaragua	4	Very good	6/2/2020
Flor de Cana Gran Res. 7	Nicaragua	7	Top of the line	2/15/2021
Frigate Reserve	Panama	8	Acceptable	4/19/2023
Gosling Black Seal	Bermuda	?	Truly a sipping Rum	8/9/2015
Grander	Panama	8	Well balanced, Slight alcohol bite	5/19/2022
Havana Club White	Cuba	3	Very good	5/5/2014
Havana Club	Cuba	7	Beautiful Rum	1/3/2022
Havana Club	Puerto Rico	?	Good	9/18/2016

Brand	Origin	Age	Comment	Date
Inmortal	Colombia	12	Nice Mellow Rum	10/25/2023
John Watlings	Nassau	3	Tastes like 100 proof Bourbon	5/19/2022
Kaniche Perfeccion	Barbedos/France	?	Blend Sweet	12/30/2018
Kaniche Reserve	Barbedos/France	?	Sweet	3/29/2021
Kaniche XO	Barbedos/France	?	Sweet	2/17/2020
Kirk & Sweeney	Dom. Rep.	18	Smooth, too sweet	2/17/2020
Marti Authentico	Panama	3	OK	8/4/2021
Mount Gay 1740	Barbados	?	Very Good	*no entry*
Mount Gay Black Barrel	Barbados	?	Robust, Full flavor, like Brandy	7/29/2020
Mount Gay Eclipse	Barbados	?	Real rum, a true rum standard	5/5/2014
Mount Gay Navy Strength	Barbados	?	114 Proof - Great with touch of soda	6/19/2024
Mount Gay XO	Barbados	?	Top quality but at a price $64	2/17/2020
Myers Single Barrel Select	Jamaica	?	Rich & heavy typical Myers flavor	10/25/2023
Navy Bay	Jamaica	?	A bit rich	2/17/2020
Old Brigand Black Label	Barbados	?	Very good	5/8/2016
Old Monk	India	7	Rough, no rum taste	1/25/2021
One Drop	Bahamas	10	Does not have Rum taste	5/19/2022
Papa's Pilar	Guyana	?	OK	5/8/2016
Papa's Pyrat	Anguilla	?	a bit of a bite	*no entry*
Pin Drop	Nassau	10	A bit spicey	9/21/2023
Plantation 5	Barbados	5	Nice flavor, alcohol bite	9/23/2022
Plantation Double Barrel	Fiji Islands	3	Taste of spice, too sweet	1/3/2022
Plantation Club XO	Barbados/France	?	Very Good, Balanced, smooth	3/29/2021
Plantation Dark Original	Barbados	?	Smooth, Rich	5/26/2021
Pompero Anniversio	Venezuela	?	Very good rum	9/3/2020
Porteno	Colombia	8	Mild, mid grade	2/17/2020
Pusser's British Navy Rum	Guyana	?	Sharp, and rich	8/4/2021
R. L. Seales	Barbados	?	Nice Rum flavor	4/30/2015
Real McCoy 12	Barbados	12	Very Good, Best of Tasting	1/25/2021
Real McCoy 5	Barbados	5	Top quality	6/20/2020
Richland Classic Res.	Georgia	?	Sharp and not worth $53	1/25/2021
Ron Cartavio	Peru	5	Good sipper	4/19/2023
Ron del Barrilito	Puerto Rico	?	Strong Vanilla & a bite	10/25/2023
Ron Matusalem 10	Dom. Rep.	10	Too Rich with heavy caramel	2/17/2020
Ron Matusalem 18	Dom. Rep.	18	Stable, mellow full bodied	5/26/2021
Ron Matusalem Gran Res.	Dom. Rep.	15	Nice treat for end of day	5/5/2014
Ron Medellin	Colombia	8	Unique flavor, fruity	1/25/2021
Ron Vizcaya Cask 12	Dom. Rep.	?	Light & Subtle	5/8/2016
Ron Zamoya	Guatamala	?	Full Body, Good	11/29/2021
Ron Zacapa Edicion Negra	Guatamala	?	Very good, smooth	5/26/2021
Ron Zacapa 23 Solera	Guatamala	?	Nice flavor, earthy	6/2/2020
Ron Zacapa XO	Guatamala	?	Good, but not $150 good	4/19/2023
Santa Teresa Ron Anejo	Venezuela	?	Good, Slightly sharp	1/25/2021
SantaTeresa 1796	Venezuela	?	Good, milder than Anejo	7/29/2020
Schooner Man's Daughter	Florida	?	Sweet	5/26/2021
Smuggler's Notch	Jeffersonville VT	3	Surprisingly smooth, tasty	1/3/2022
Starr	Mauritius Isle	7	Good rum	5/26/2021
Zaya	Trinidad	5+16	Rich, sweet	8/4/2021

Made in United States
Troutdale, OR
12/27/2024

27335646R00197